Finding

Peace

Finding Peace

By

Jack Roberts

May this book serve humanity by helping individuals
to view the world in a more compassionate,
peaceful way.

May this have a ripple effect that reaches out to
everyone.

May we be united by our similarities and common
humanity, rather than divided by our differences.

Published by Jack Roberts

www.finding-peace.co.uk

NOTE: The material contained in this book is derived from personal opinions and provided in good faith for general guidance but no liability can be accepted for loss or expense incurred as a result of relying in particular circumstances on statements made in the book. Readers should consider their own personal circumstances and check situations with relevant, appropriately-qualified professionals rather than relying on material or suggestions contained within this book.

ISBN: 9781532872525

Contents

Preface

I'm not a trained psychologist or religious leader. I haven't spent years meditating in a cave or suffered for years at the hands of brutal captors and found peace afterwards. I'm just an ordinary man who has suffered from anxiety and depression, drank too much at periods of my life, had both joyful and failed relationships, been successful in some jobs and failed in others. I've loved people which has sometimes been returned and sometimes not, plus I've been proud and arrogant then knocked off my perch to the satisfaction of others. My health is generally good but now in middle-age things feel like they're beginning to drop off or fail me. I've had loved ones die of illness and others who I've had to look after. I've had my house and car broken into on several occasions, I've been mugged and was bullied as a child.

All my immediate blood family are dead - my brother to alcoholism at 42, dad to a heart attack at 65 and my mother to cancer at 70 after prolonged illnesses, plus all my aunts and uncles at various ages. I have an ex-partner who committed suicide. I've been divorced although I am now happily re-married but I don't have any children. I've never been in a major car accident, disabled, tortured, sexually or physically abused, badly beaten, imprisoned or hospitalised for anything more than routine operations. So I have a wide range of personal experiences, some wonderful and many unpleasant, but nothing you probably haven't also had, to a greater or lesser degree.

This book is the result of a journey. Like everyone else on the planet, I have my hang-ups, fears and worries. I've always been interested in self-help and psychology and have studied both looking for 'the answer'. I have spent over one thousand pounds on therapy and investigated religion. None of them truly gave the 'answer' but all of them gave me something, although some more than others. What I've now realized is that they **couldn't** give me the answer because none of them **had** it, they only had bits of it, like individual jigsaw pieces. It was up to me to put the jigsaw together, which is what this book represents.

Over the last few years I have assembled the jigsaw pieces into a picture that works for me. It represents a framework that helps to release me from many of the hang-ups, fears and anxieties I have, giving me a sense of happiness and peace – or at least an understanding of why things are the way they are, and why I am the way I am.

I can't promise that my framework and view of the world will help you. But I do hope it helps you see which jigsaw pieces are most relevant for you and how you might assemble them in a more helpful way.

Introduction

This book is split into two parts.

The first part provides an overview of my thoughts on why the world is the way it is. We tend to think of the world as a static, fixed object that somehow owes us something, that if we do the right things it will give us what we want and expect. We think of it as something we are born into, then have to follow a set of rules in order to live successfully within it. It's as if the world is out there waiting for us and we then develop a series of expectations towards it. We say; 'if only we do the right thing, it will be kind to us'. I think this is an unhelpful way to view the world. Instead, the world is a living, dynamic organism that evolves based on what happens to the things and people within it and what everyone does. There are no 'rules for life'. The only real rule is that all actions have consequences, and this is what makes the world that we see around us. This first part presents the 'big picture'.

The first part also looks at our place within the world and how we have become what we are. It looks at what has made us the way we are and how our actions and thoughts create consequences that then govern our lives.

The second part explores some routes for

living in a happier, more contented and peaceful way. It picks up the theme of consequences and effects and shows how we can move more towards actions and thoughts that lead to a more fulfilling life, including some techniques to aid the process along.

Many of us believe that it is possible to control life, but I believe this is a great misconception. Instead, life controls us. But this isn't a negative message, it's actually very hopeful. Rather than trying to make things happen in a certain way because we believe it will bring us happiness, we can instead open to what life presents to us, but in a more accepting and understanding way.

One of our big problems is expectations. We expect things to happen in a certain way because it's what we want to happen, then get disappointed when it doesn't turn out like that. But the problem isn't really how it turned out, it's that we expected and hoped it would be different.

This might sound like a very passive approach where we resign ourselves to everything rather than trying to make the world a better place or 'improve' ourselves, but it isn't. Instead, if we have an understanding of the way cause and effect works, we can see the consequences of approaches and then move more towards those which will bring beneficial outcomes. So it's actually very active and positive. It's about understanding and applying wisdom, rather than trying to control the uncontrollable and getting disappointed at the inevitable result.

We are told that if we work hard, pass exams, get a job, career, house, partner and all the other things society promises, then we'll be happy and everything will be fine. What we're not told is that it will lead to stress, anxiety, depression, excessive pressure and lost opportunities. We strive for things hoping that they will make everything 'right' but then get disappointed when we don't get what we want, or lose it, or the novelty wears off, or we see someone with a better 'something' than we have. Bitterness, jealousy, anger and upset are the inevitable results of this.

It doesn't occur to us in any way that we might be responsible for what we see and experience around us, or what happens to us. We feel that the world happens **to** us, rather than **because** of us. This is also what the concepts of fate or destiny indicate, as if everything is pre-ordained and our job is to live it out.

An alternative view is that we might be responsible for creating the world around us. What we personally experience and see in the world is a direct consequence of what we feel inside and what we do. What we see around us in the world is a consequence of the actions of those within it – including ourselves. So we have to take personal responsibility for what happens and what we choose to do. It isn't anyone's 'fault', everything is a consequence of an action and our responsibility lies in what we create and how we react to what is created around us.

We can see how these cause and effect relationships work when applied to actions, speech and thoughts. If you say something, it will have a consequence. Loving, caring speech has a positive effect whereas negative, divisive gossip creates an unpleasant atmosphere. If your mind is downhearted and full of negativity, then everything you see around you will appear to back up this view. On the other hand, if your thoughts are joyful and peaceful, that's how you will see and perceive the world. Everything looks better on a sunny day when you're rested or on holiday.

If you drop a cup, it breaks. The cup didn't break because of fate or destiny, it was simply a consequence of dropping the cup, caused by gravity. If you walk out in front of a bus you'll get hit by it. It's not caused by a mysterious, external force or bad luck, it's a consequence of actions.

The way we perceive the world will also determine how we relate to it. If we perceive the world as harsh, then we will see harsh and unpleasant things around us that verify our opinion. If we are joyful, then we can spend hours getting pleasure from a daisy that other people wouldn't even see, or would tread on without giving it a second thought.

This overall way of viewing the world is like a giant, lifelong puzzle which doesn't really have an answer. Instead, it's a method of relating to the world that helps us to understand more about why it is the way it is, and why different things happen to us. It needs to be returned to again and again throughout our life and thought about in different ways, otherwise we will get caught up in the problems of the world. We will be caught up *in* the world, rather than relating to it in a more helpful, peaceful, understanding way.

A key point to remember here is that the way we relate to the world, i.e. our perceptions and understanding of causes and associated effects, might not actually make the world any different. But it *feels* different because of the way we relate to it. Happiness, sadness, anger and other such concepts are internal feelings which we can work with in order to view the world differently, rather than trying to change the things around us.

I wish this way of viewing the world had been explained to me when I was still a child, rather than society and school sending me down the 'do the right thing' path. I call this approach '*The Great Swindle*', but that's perhaps an incorrect term as it implies intention. No-one (parents, society, teachers, etc.) deliberately sends us down an unhelpful path, they just don't know any better and are only following what they themselves were taught. Perhaps it could be called '*The Great Travesty*' instead, as it's very sad.

Sailing can provide us with an analogy for the way we live in the world. Being in a dinghy going in a straight line when the water is smooth and someone has set the sail for us is easy. But when the wind changes direction or the water gets choppy we will struggle and feel adrift. We might then blame the weather or the boat or ourselves for being incompetent, but this is wrong. The real problem isn't that the weather changed or that we are useless, it's that we were never taught how to sail.

So we don't know how to react to choppier water or a change in wind direction. It's like being told that everything will be fine and then we realize it isn't but don't know what to do. If we are taught to sail then we will have no worries about the weather or water. We understand the mechanics of it and know what to do when circumstances change and things don't go to plan.

Our upbringing is the same. We are set out on a path but not taught the appropriate rules for living, meaning that we're not taught how to live effectively. So when our life doesn't go to plan, we blame everything else rather than realizing that we were never taught how to live in a more helpful and effective way. It isn't anyone's fault, no-one has done anything 'wrong', but when we do realize that we are in this situation it's up to us to find a way out, to learn how to live more appropriately and get more out of life. This book and the principles contained within it can help if you do find yourself adrift.

Part One

Understanding Our World

This part of the book examines how the world we perceive is formed and how we as an individual have become who we are. Understanding both aspects are important as they give us a picture of why we are the way we are and why we experience the world way we do.

The first chapter demonstrates how the state of the world is a function of those within it. It follows, therefore, that if we wish to know more about the world and how it operates, we need to examine ourselves. We both influence the world around us and it influences us too. So the other chapters in this section provide guidance and tools on how to examine ourselves, and how to see who we have become and why. With this knowledge we can assess whether we are happy with it, or need to make changes. By knowing how we became the way we are, we will be in an excellent position to know how to make it different.

The world doesn't exist in the way we think it does. We have the impression of having been born into a static, unchanging object with rules that we have to work within. But it isn't like that. Instead, it's actually a continuously changing, dynamic organism that will evolve based on what the people of the world say, think and do.

The first chapter explores some of the wider aspects of this to give the 'big picture'. A big picture makes sense when looked at from a distance but begins to become a bit fuzzy when viewed close-up. So the first chapter shows how the wider world in which we live has evolved and continues to evolve, with subsequent chapters allowing you to delve into the detail of the big picture, i.e. you and your place in it.

Chapter 1

An Evolving World

A question many people ask is why 'God' allows such terrible things as earthquakes, tsunamis, floods, volcanoes and the like, and why 'he' allows wars and other horrific actions committed by humans on other humans. But if you look at the history of the world and the universe, these events have always been there. Our planet has been convulsed with earthquakes, floods, asteroid strikes and all manner of other events for the billions of years it has been in existence for.

Britain itself was created by a major flood and tsunami that split the island off from the rest of continental Europe. It didn't come from an external force or entity, it came about through the natural convulsion of the earth that we walk upon. If it were not for volcanoes, the nutrients that the land needed to generate plant growth and keep us alive would never have happened. The problem isn't that these things happen, it's that we don't expect them to happen so don't allow for it. So we build homes in flood plains and live in earthquake zones without adequate protection and then get shocked when they do happen.

It's as if we have this need to blame everything

that happens on an external source, rather than realizing that they are an inevitable consequence of life on this planet. This doesn't mean we shouldn't show compassion for people caught up in these tragic events, we should. It is an important part of our basic humanity to look after those less fortunate than ourselves or who are caught up in terrible circumstances. But it does demonstrate a fundamental lack of understanding of the way the world is.

Wars and the other horrific acts that we inflict on each other don't come from some external source, such as 'evil' or the 'devil', they come from us. They happen in the world as a result of what we as people do. If we look deep within our hearts we will often see that there is a lot of bitterness, anger and resentment there. We focus on our needs and want them met, even if that is at the expense of others. This is the root of all conflict.

Wars and atrocities come directly from these human feelings, but on a larger scale than just our own feelings. Our own personal views and feelings get magnified by society so that a whole community can reflect that way of thinking, leading to some societies feeling that it is okay to commit atrocities for its own ends. All wars and international disagreements come directly from this way of thinking, magnified to a society or country level. Hitler and other dictators could only come to power because their societies allowed it to happen, at some level. As the saying goes;

"*the only thing necessary for the triumph of evil is for good people to do nothing*".

Role Models

Your past role models will determine how you currently see the world and present ones will determine how you perceive the world in the years to come. You are also a role model for everyone around you and who comes after you. So choose carefully and be aware of the messages you give.

Children and young people usually can't pick their role models or most of the people in their environment. They can't choose parents, family, school, society, or the place they live. But these are all highly important aspects of our development and growth as a person. What we encounter from these groups as a child, teenager and youth, will determine how we view the world as an adult.

If we are brought up in a loving, caring, supportive environment then it is likely that we will either view the world as an inherently loving and benevolent place, or we will feel entitled to the best things the world can offer – because that's what we had as a child.

If we are brought up in a violent, angry or anxious environment then it is very likely that we will feel the world is a harsh, uncaring place that needs to be beaten and conquered. Our softer side will not be shown as that could indicate vulnerability, which will then be pounced upon and punished by the 'world'. Alternatively, we may go the opposite way and be compassionate and sensitive. Having experienced harshness and feeling pain, we never want others to experience the same thing.

Sometimes we think traits such as anxiety, depression and addictive behaviours, or alternatively a loving, caring, compassionate nature, are in our genes. But perhaps they aren't. Maybe they are actually a direct result of what we experienced during our upbringing. We have, in effect, modelled the behaviours and thought patterns of those we were brought up with, by, and around. There may be a predisposition towards certain personality traits, but they need to be activated to become our nature as an adult. This is why our role models are so important – they shape our view of the world.

We can't change who our role models were, but we can identify and understand what they gave us and what we acquired from them. This knowledge is not an excuse to blame our parents or anyone else. Just like you, they have also modelled behaviours from their own societies, upbringing, environments and circumstances. Instead, you can use it to identify the aspects of your behaviour and personality that are helpful, and what isn't. Remember also that these aspects aren't you, they have merely been picked up as you have gone through life. As they have been acquired rather than necessarily being an inherent part of your nature, you can change them – but you need to have identified them first.

We can also use this knowledge to find more appropriate role models and mentors, i.e. those that exhibit traits which create happier, more peaceful and less stressed lives.

We are also role models for those around us. People around us will reflect and respond to our behaviour, so if you don't want an angry, unhappy environment, then make sure you aren't creating that type of atmosphere around you. How will you know if you are? Look at your role models from childhood. What kind of atmosphere did they create? You could be doing exactly the same but don't realize it. A society's rules and values are created by the modelled behaviour of everyone within the community, but it can also create them too.

If you've ever been to a football match you'll know how the atmosphere seems to get picked up by everyone in the ground. It can often have a very aggressive, testosterone-fueled vibe to it. This feeling then becomes self-fueling. The more aggressive and worked up everyone gets, the more aggressive and worked up they seem to become, including those on the pitch.

Contrast this with the audience watching a classical music concert accompanied by fireworks in the grounds of a stately home. Everyone is relaxed and happy with picnic hampers on the grass enjoying the evening. There may be the same number of people at both events, but the atmosphere is very, very different.

The lesson from this is that we pick up on society's attitudes and the group culture around us. We might usually be a very calm and relaxed person but get caught up in the atmosphere of the big match, or we can be racked with anxiety but still find a few hours peace at the concert.

This group culture applies not only to major events, it also relates to the day-to-day company we keep, such as our friends and family, work colleagues and the neighbourhood in which we live. It also extends to regions, countries, continents and religions. Our leaders in these areas create a society, a group culture, which we then take as 'right'.

Residents of countries tend to think in a certain way, which is where our stereotypes come from. The words Scotsman, Spaniard, Englishman, Afghani, Frenchman, Indian and Italian all conjure up images of the people within the country. Scots have a very distinct way of viewing the world, which is different from the way an Afghan woman would view the world. Neither is right or wrong, they're just different. They are products of their society. Their view of the world and how it operates is determined by their society – so is yours.

We can look at who we consider to be 'successful' in our society as a mirror for what we consider right or good. In the UK, we admire TV programmes such as *The Apprentice, Jeremy Kyle, The X-Factor* and *Big Brother.* A fundamental part of these programmes is the humiliation that comes with failure. They are designed in such a way that people strive for achievement but only some of them can succeed, which creates the opportunity to judge and humiliate those who don't. We create the impression that achievement is all that matters, that success can be achieved without hard work (reality TV celebrities) and that to 'fail' (or not succeed) is a bad thing. This creates phenomenal pressure on us as individuals to act in a certain way, or we will also feel humiliated for our apparent 'failure' or lack of success.

Examples of those we consider to be successful people could be premier league footballers with their tantrums and arrogance who cheat via diving in order to win a game. Or CEOs of major corporations who could just as easily have become murderous psychopaths if they had a tendency towards violence and hadn't used their intelligence for business purposes. The lack of empathy and consideration for others whilst striving to 'win' at all costs are similar characteristics to many violent criminals, but as the CEO has made lots of money for shareholders or themselves, we view them as a success and emulate them as role models.

The world seems to be a harsh, tough, competitive place because our role models are the people that exhibit these characteristics, rather than those who care and are compassionate. Our society is more focused on earning money than it is in looking after the old (who are generally more wise than the young) or the weak such as disabled children who can't fend for themselves. We reward those who win at the expense of others, rather than those who care about others. We give bankers large bonuses, rather than rewarding those who clean incontinent, disabled old people or impart wisdom and guidance to our children or look after them whilst we are trying to earn money.

Trying to 'succeed' when success is defined in these ways will ultimately lead only to pain and hardship. There may be short term gains in the form of wealth or achievement, but eventually it will create a feeling of disappointment and 'something missing'. We'll never quite succeed 'enough', because we'll always be striving for something else, because that's what our society encourages us to do.

Our society, the leaders we select (or allow, as a group, to take over) and our own personal actions create the world we see around us. All of these are our role models – and it's not always pretty.

Separation, Discrimination and Perception

We instinctively see the world in terms of 'this' and 'that'. We are different from that person and that tree is not the same object as this car.

That all sounds fairly obvious. But the problem lies in what it leads to. By discriminating between this and that, we introduce perception, or how we feel about it. We like this person, but not that one. It's a 'bad' car when it breaks down but a 'good' tree when it blooms in the spring. This way of viewing the world seems to be ingrained within us. We cannot think of another way that the world could possibly be. But it's actually at the root of many problems.

We spend our life trying to get more of what we perceive as good and avoid what we perceive as bad. But none of it is accurate, as our perceptions are formed from our personal life experiences, our role models, and the society in which we live. What we think of as good now, may be bad in a few years' time. We may love our partner and want to spend the rest of our lives with them, but then the relationship breaks down and the marriage ends in acrimony and hatred. We love the new car, until it too breaks down.

We also attribute qualities to things that aren't deserved. We might refer to our 'bad' back or 'dodgy' knee, for example. But the reality is that the back isn't 'bad', it's just a back. We might have mistreated it by working it too hard or perhaps have had an injury. But none of this makes it 'bad'. Sore, yes, but not 'bad', as if it were naughty. It's as if we have an expectation that things should go a certain way and when they don't, we blame them. So the back is bad because it didn't do what we wanted. Or something is 'wrong' with the car

19

because it isn't working as effectively as it used to.

But look a little deeper at these examples. Perhaps the back is sore after giving you 50 years of faithful service but you didn't look after it properly. You may have used ineffective lifting techniques and asked it to do more than it was capable of doing. Or perhaps the car has 'gone wrong' because it hasn't had its regular service and having done 100,000 miles, some of its mechanical parts are getting a bit worn out.

We live in a world of opposites. Day and night. Light and dark. Good and evil. Right and wrong. Ancient wisdom teachings have a label for this – duality, meaning two - as opposed to 'oneness', which doesn't have these distinctions. An alternative view to this world of opposites, of duality, involves taking a more dispassionate view of things and exercising mindfulness. By being aware of how we see things, we can identify when we are exercising unhelpful perception, perhaps because we are holding on to past feelings or intolerant views. We can then consider these perceptions and where they came from, before considering whether the situation really is one of right and wrong, or perhaps is a little bit muddier than that.

You may have heard of the phrase 'at one with everything'. Normally we are 'at one' with ourselves, i.e. there's us as an individual, then there's the rest of the universe, and we're separate. I'm me and the world is the world. I might be **in** the world, but I'm still only **a part** of it, separate from everything else, with everything having its own unique identity and existence.

Being 'at one with everything' removes this distinction so that we don't see ourselves as merely part of the world, as if we were a visitor. Instead, we realize that we are intricately tied up with everything that has happened, everything that is happening, and everything that will happen. We are an integral part of its overall evolution and development. We aren't separate from anything, we are intimately joined to it and everything in it. We can then see and experience everything and everyone the way they really are, i.e. as bundles of actions evolving however the consequences of their actions takes them, without discrimination or prejudice towards them. This knowledge allows us to understand the world. This **is** the set of rules for operating in the world that you've been looking for all your life.

This is a key area in understanding how we see the world. By understanding why we see the world the way we do, it can help us interpret it differently. We can experience it in a way which is more helpful, peaceful and joyful.

An analogy for the concept of separation and discrimination is to think of weather. We view the weather forecast on television and look for 'our' weather. But where does the weather start and end? It doesn't. It is a continuous, endlessly flowing cycle of change with multiple aspects affecting everything else, everywhere. If there is a hurricane in the Gulf of Mexico, it will affect the weather in the UK, which will also affect the weather in Europe which will also be affected by the jet stream which is influenced by conditions in Asia, and so on. Continuous and ever–changing, endlessly.

We might view the hurricane as having a start and end point, but these are just convenient labels to describe a set of conditions, they're not real. The hurricane arises in the Atlantic as a result of weather conditions and then grows based on the conditions. Meteorologists watch these changing conditions and at some point might declare them as 'hurricane', but this is an arbitrary decision. We could change the definition so that it wasn't called a hurricane any more, but the weather conditions themselves wouldn't have changed one bit. We may say that the hurricane has finished, but it hasn't, it's actually transformed into something else and remnants of it will hang around for a time in other places, such as in the UK. It might not be raining as heavily or as windy, but when did it actually 'stop'? It stopped at the point we defined it as having stopped. We could change our definitions, then it would neither have started nor stopped as it would be seen as a never-ending stream of changing conditions.

Another example of this is the world's oceans. If you look at a map of the world then it is quite easy to see where the Atlantic ends and the Pacific or Indian Ocean begins. But it's not really that simple.

There isn't a sign in the middle of the sea with a label on it saying 'Welcome to the Pacific Ocean'. The water in the two oceans is constantly intermingling and affecting each other, together with the effects of atmospheric conditions and surrounding landmasses. The only way you'd know that you'd crossed from the Atlantic to the Pacific is because the map tells you that you have. The label for where you are may have changed, but the reality hasn't as you're still in a boat in a continuous mass of water that looks identical to the apparently different ocean you've just come from.

If you're next to a tree you might call it 'this tree' and call the tree over there 'that tree'. But if you walked over to 'that tree' the tree you were at originally – which was called 'this tree' - would now be called 'that tree'. You've changed its name and identity based on where you are, because it suits your purpose. But are the two trees really that separate? They both have roots stretching into the same patch of ground, share the same earth and history, the same water and the same sun, with roots of plants and grasses intertwined all the way between the two trees. They may be separate in our vision, but they are actually interlinked and interdependent on each other, with many similar causes and conditions.

So how does this help us? Well, look at your children. Where did they come from? From you. Where did they get their personalities and ways of viewing the world? From you. Where did they get their friends? From the schools you sent them to. But remember also that their birth and upbringing will have changed your attitudes and circumstances quite dramatically too, so your own views of the world are dependent and interlinked with them and their actions. Your children also get their views and attitudes from society, as did you, so again we are all interlinked through the interactions of society. Everyone alive today and who has ever lived is part of this process and is thus interlinked and interconnected with everyone else who has ever lived on the planet, to a greater or lesser degree.

Looking in this way helps us to see how similar we all are. We might not all look or talk the same, but the path to how we got to our current position in life is the same, i.e. from parents, wider society, and history. We often focus on the differences between us, particularly if we look at different nations, cultures or religions, but it's amazing just how similar and interconnected we all are. Thich Nhat Hanh, The Vietnamese Buddhist monk and Nobel Peace Prize nominee, uses the term 'interbeing' to describe this concept. He claims that a realization of our interbeing is needed if we are to survive and evolve as a species. We can try to recognize our dependency on everyone and everything else, and realize how much our histories and futures are intimately tied up with each other.

We may discriminate, categorise, label and

form judgements, but we need this ability in order to live in the world and communicate with each other. The danger is when we start to live our lives based on these judgements and labels. We get attached to the label of our nation, culture, society, opinions, religion or identity and fight to preserve it, protect it, promote it, 'for the common good'. But it's all just labels. Like the hurricane, we define and label it in order to attach some kind of reality to it. Then it's a solid 'thing' that we can latch on to and understand. We think we have 'knowledge' because we've been able to discriminate and label.

But if you change the label or its definition, it changes what you see as 'reality'. Many of the world's human-based problems are caused by people labelling and judging, then putting effort into promoting and preserving the labels, or more accurately their personal meaning behind the labels. We could solve many of the world's problems if we stopped labelling and started to see beyond the label to what unites, rather than using it to separate and discriminate.

This isn't merely a plea for world peace and unity, it's an explanation of the way the world is. Look at how you view your family, friends, neighbours and work colleagues to see how much discriminating and judging you do. They're a pain, he's a good person. The only 'pain' or 'good' they actually have is what we attach to them, and that's down to our perception. It might be based on our experience or their behaviour, but that **is** what we base our perceptions, and therefore judgements, on. Aim for understanding rather than discriminating and judging, then watch how your view of the world changes as a result. We experience our world the way we do because we separate and discriminate, then judge what we see and respond by trying to control it.

If you think about how the world currently looks, all the pain and hardship and unpleasantness, you can trace it back to this sequence of separation and discrimination, judgement and control. But you won't be able to find the precise starting point, because it has been evolving like this forever. The only way it can be stopped is for you to stop reacting in this way and do something differently. You can't change the whole world, but you can change yourself. By extension, everyone you know or come into contact with will also change as a result – but don't try to force or make others change. Everyone has to change themselves, all you can do is be a role model.

Areas for Contemplation

- ◆ Do you wonder why 'God' allows terrible disasters to happen?

- ◆ Are you believer in fate or destiny? How do

you believe they work? Do you and your family feel blessed, cursed or unlucky?

♦ Who are your current role models? Who were your past role models and what do you believe they have given you?

♦ Do you view the world as inherently benevolent, or is it a dangerous place?

♦ Are you a believer in a strong society or do you favour the rights of the individual?

♦ Do you consider yourself judgmental and opinionated? Do you know anyone who is?

♦ Do you often engage in general debate or do your discussions generally feel more argumentative?

♦ Would you be willing to die for any causes or concepts such as your family, city, region, country, religion, politics or home? How do you personally define each of these and has that definition changed over time?

Chapter 2

Analysing our Personality

We tend to view the world and everything associated with it as 'out there', external to us. Fate, destiny, luck, God's judgement, 'our cross to bear' are all ways of viewing the world, but they are seen as something imposed on us from outside. When we have a disagreement or problem with someone, we think it's *they* who are the problem, not us. So we tend to spend our time trying to control external events and things. We try to bend them to what we want or make them into something they aren't.

If we have a problem with someone, the problem is actually with **us**, not them. They might be causing us problems, but it's not a problem for them as they are just being themselves. They might not have a problem, but **we** do. Our problem is that we cannot cope with them being themselves. We expect them to be something other than they actually are, or think they 'should' do something, just because we want or expect it. And **that** is the problem we have. It's not necessarily what they do that causes the problem, it's that it's different from what we expect or want, and that expectation lies within us.

The issue is that we externalize everything, rather than taking personal responsibility for our own thoughts, feelings and actions. We might have grown up with these ways of being and not known any other way, but that doesn't mean it's right. It merely means we don't realize how we act or the true consequences of what we do.

Some things will happen because we choose to go down a certain path, e.g. the career decisions we make or where we decide to live, but others will happen to us, such as cars breaking down, accidents, or a house being burgled. We can't do anything about these external events – other than to choose our reaction to them. We can get bitter and angry, or accepting and patient. One leads to upset and depression, the other leads to a more peaceful and happy outlook on life. This is taking personal responsibility for our feelings, thoughts and emotions, rather than externalizing them or blaming someone or something else.

There is a concept from Buddhism that explains this very well. Buddhism says that it's as if we have been shot with two arrows. The first arrow is the event itself, the external thing that happens to us. We can't do anything about this. But we fire the second arrow into ourselves by the way we respond and react to the event. By bemoaning the unfairness of it all and getting angry and bitter or wanting revenge, we relive the event and its pain over and over again. We don't have to react this way, we can act differently. Additional suffering from the event is our decision, the path we choose.

Another traditional Buddhist way of looking at this is to imagine trying to walk across a patch of ground full of thorns and thistles. You could try and pull out all the thorns or even pave it over. Alternatively, you could put on a pair of thick, sturdy boots and simply walk across. The traditional way of viewing the world is the former approach – trying to change the ground – whereas it's easier to simply put boots on. But you have to put your own boots on, no-one else will do it for you. You have to take personal responsibility.

The opposite of personal responsibility is externalizing problems. Rather than looking at our own reactions, thoughts and actions, we blame everything that happens on something or someone else, external to us. It's our upbringing, or genes, or people's lack of understanding, or the weather, or the unfairness of life, or the government, or the economy, or lack of opportunity, or our parents and family, or our boss. In fact, anything *but* us. External things do happen and expecting anything else is only ever going to lead to disappointment. But we can examine our reactions to it, and how we may have influenced or created it.

We can spot this happening when people say things like 'who's fault is it?', or saying that everything would be fine if only everyone else changed what they do or did something different. The root of this approach is separation, as was discussed in the 'Separation, Discrimination and Perception' section of Chapter 1. There's us, and then there's everyone else. We fail to see our connections and interdependence with everything in the world so naturally externalize things as being 'something else', not us.

We also look to the external world to give us happiness or release us from our pain. So we take medication, or alcohol, or drugs, or look to relationships to 'complete' us. But the only way to true, long-lasting peace, happiness and contentment is to look inside ourselves and find our peace and sense of completeness there. This doesn't mean we detach ourselves from the external world – we can't, we're intricately bound up with it. But having an understanding of causes and effects together with an appreciation of the consequences of our own actions and thoughts allows us to see the differences between something we need to learn to deal with, and what we might be able to do something about.

Spending a life externalizing means we will never be happy as there's always something to blame, always a reason why things don't go the way we want them to or the way we think they should. Nothing will ever be good enough for us and we will never be happy because we are relying on something outside of us to go a certain way. But we can't control the external world, it will evolve the way it is going to evolve and we will always be at its mercy if we rely on it to meet our needs. Externalization is a route to permanent disappointment, unhappiness and a feeling of things never quite being good enough and always problematic.

We can use an example to see how not appreciating the cause and effect reality of the world affects us. Imagine you are waiting at a set of traffic lights one morning in your car and someone bumps into you from behind. If we were feeling angry or irritated before the bump happened we might get annoyed and angry with the person who crashed into us. But if we were feeling calm at the time our reaction is likely to be more measured. We won't be happy at what has happened, it still creates inconvenience and possibly expense, but it is less likely to disturb our peace of mind.

But we can look at it even more deeply. Think about why the person crashed into us. If we are angry then we are likely to blame them for being careless, incompetent, or a useless driver, all of which fuels our anger. But perhaps the other person has also had a bad day. Perhaps they have just found out that their teenage daughter is taking drugs or was the victim of sexual abuse. Perhaps they were also facing potential redundancy that day and were worried about what might happen. Maybe they themselves were also the victim of sexual abuse as a child and they are racked with anxiety and guilt about it. A whole host of different things may be going on that led to the lack of attention which ultimately led to you having a bit of inconvenience. Add your own anger and frustration into this and you create a very volatile mixture.

So what happens next? Do you accept the situation or react with anger towards the other person? In that situation is your anger going to inflame or calm the situation? Who's fault is it? The abusers from childhood? Society that fuels anxiety? The endless pressure to work and achieve? The busy roads? The traffic lights that didn't change quick enough? It's all of these things and none of them. It's simply a result of cause and effect, leading to the events of that moment.

We can trace all of history back as a series of causes and effects in an unbroken line, all of them leading to this moment and also creating the future. The future will be created by what happens now, i.e. our reactions to current events. And that's what we take personal responsibility for – our part in the sequence of cause and effect and our reactions to it.

The other person may or may not take personal responsibility for what happened, but that's not our concern. We can't change them or what they do, only ourselves. Trying to get other people to take personal responsibility is an attempt to control the external world and will only ever lead to upset and disappointment. This doesn't mean we don't try and change things, but we can only change those things which are under our control – our actions and reactions.

The Road Less Travelled by M. Scott Peck presents a useful framework for assessing whether we take personal responsibility or have a tendency to blame others. It says that people fall on a spectrum from neurotic (it's all my fault) to character-disordered (it's everyone else's fault). Individuals generally gravitate to one end of the spectrum rather than gather around the middle.

A neurotic is likely to suffer from issues such as low self-esteem, guilt, or lacking in confidence. Perhaps as children they were continually blamed for problems or felt excessive pressure to achieve, or it might have been as a result of other life experiences. Neurotics take too much personal responsibility and do not feel able to do anything about their situation.

Character-disordered individuals are more likely to be arrogant and self-obsessed. 'Failure is not an option' may be a catchphrase for them and if things do not go as they wish, it will be because of something external, never their fault. They do not take any personal responsibility. Again it might have come from their upbringing and experiences, perhaps through excessive praise or never being taught self-reliance, personal responsibility and independence.

Neither of the two terms are particularly attractive labels or ways that we would like to think of ourselves. Unfortunately though, most of us do fit into one of these two categories. It is a rare individual indeed who can objectively review a situation, work out what's really going on and then take appropriate action from a position of wisdom and full understanding. Some might even say that these rare individuals were enlightened.

Rather than using these concepts of neurotic and character-disordered as another tool with which to beat yourself up, think rationally and calmly about which end of the spectrum you are most likely to fit into and the situations or instances where you might exhibit a different pattern from usual. It will help you to understand how you view the world and why you feel the way you do about certain things. Whichever end of the spectrum you fit in, it's not a problem, it's just another tool to help you understand yourself and the world you experience.

Achievement Orientation

A great scourge of our age is the 'microwave mentality' of expecting things now, rather than having to wait. We're all about getting more, doing more, being more. Our status in the eyes of the external world is seen by our success – or what we've achieved, in other words. As children we were taught what we needed to achieve and what would constitute success and lead to happiness. Because we follow what we're taught (because we don't know any better), we follow these patterns of achievement, seeking what has been defined for us as 'success'. This is the root of ambition and we tend to view it as a positive aspect, a 'good thing'. We look unfavourably on those we perceive as lacking ambition.

A consequence of this approach is that we then view the world in terms of achievement, hence why we always want more. We are never satisfied, because we are continually striving to achieve. We never seem to reach the point where we have 'achieved', job done. The rich want more money, the successful want more status, those with big houses want bigger, better houses. The beautiful want to be more beautiful so indulge in cosmetic surgery.

Is it any wonder we go through life with a feeling of dissatisfaction when the whole structure of our education and society is about achieving more? It's impossible for us to actually attain this mythical position of 'achieved' or 'success' because it doesn't really exist. And when we do get what we consider to be 'success', we then strive to keep it and not lose it – another reason why the beautiful have cosmetic anti-ageing surgery and the rich try to protect their wealth.

It's as if dissatisfaction is built in to our whole approach, because there is never a point when we have enough to be satisfied. This achievement-orientation can be incredibly destructive. Rather than enjoying what we have and what's around us, we have a perpetual feeling of 'not good enough'. Do we really want to spend our lives striving for a few moments of 'enough' before then worrying about losing it? Is it not better to take a more balanced approach rather than seeking the 'enough' feeling again but this time needing it to be bigger, stronger and better in order to achieve the same feeling?

A major downside of a strong achievement-orientation is that we fail to see what's right in front of us. We don't appreciate the moment as we're always looking for something else. We miss the joy of the sound of the rain on the window because we want to get outside and do something. We miss the joy of the freshly fallen snow because we want to get somewhere. We don't taste our food because we're busy thinking about something else.

Our children can miss out on the joy of play and the opportunity to try new things because we lead them down a path of achievement. They have to do well in their exams so they can get jobs and careers and 'make something of themselves'. They then take this into their adult lives and so the cycle continues.

The root of this feeling is a sense of being incomplete. We feel that something is missing and seek to find it, so we're striving for more all the time and never really appreciating what we have. We actually need very little to be happy and we are already complete as we are. We only feel that we're not complete because society tells us that we need more, that the partner, car, latest phone, bigger house, better job will somehow complete us and create happiness. It won't, it'll merely make us want more, meaning we spend our lives wanting.

I'm not suggesting that we need to remove ambition or desire. What I'm saying is that the endless striving creates unhappiness and a feeling of lack. We could instead appreciate what's around us and what we have, so that whatever we get *adds* to our happiness, rather than believing it to be the cause of it.

Those with a strong achievement-orientation often concentrate on getting things completed. This is useful for finishing a job as the end result is always in focus, but we miss the joy of actually doing the task. It's hard to become a great artist or achieve mastery of anything with an achievement-orientation because we take pleasure in ticking the job as complete, rather than the joy of doing it. We paint to have a finished picture, not for the joy of painting. We learn to play the piano to achieve a mythical position of 'now I can play' and miss the fact that 'playing the piano' means actually sitting down and doing it. The joy can come from the playing and doing, often more so than the temporary pleasure gained from achieving.

We are taught that we can have it all. If we do the right things and set our mind to it, we can have everything we want. This is an inappropriate approach for two reasons. First of all, we don't know what the future holds and it may not allow the thing we are striving for. We might have an accident, for example, or someone else gets the job we want. Secondly, we miss out on other things and continue an unhelpful cycle. We are taught, for example, that it is okay to have a career and work full time whilst bringing up children, that we can 'have it all'. Perhaps this can be achieved by contracting-out the child care, but it's worth considering what the other potential impacts of that might be.

We might actually be showing children that it is okay to contract-out their care and that our parents might be more interested in providing for themselves and their own needs, rather than being with their children. By working and earning we may be teaching children that being able to buy more things is more important than spending time with family members and loved ones. Perhaps we're showing them that it is okay to contract-out love and caring, which may come back and bite us when we need their support as we get older. But we've taught them that it's more important to work and earn than look after family and spend time with them.

When our children leave home are we likely to think; 'I'm glad I spent time working and earning'? We are more likely to wish that we had spent more time with them whilst we could. We realize the time was precious as they grew up so quickly – but we missed the chance. The children may also think that they themselves are less important than working and earning – achieving – so we give them a legacy of low self-esteem and anxiety about their career performance and whether they are achieving enough, because that's what our actions have taught them is important.

Children do ask for material goods which drives parents to work harder, especially when the children see their friends with the latest goods and gadgets, or organizing bigger and better parties than their peers. But ultimately what our children really want from us is our time. They want parents to spend time with them. It doesn't even matter what we do necessarily, so long as we are with them. Some of the finest presents I've ever seen – both for children and adults – came from a loved one spending time with someone. Not an object, but time and shared experiences. This is what we'll remember when they leave home, rather than the objects we bought for them.

It is hard to bring up children in a materialistic world. It drives us to work harder and sometimes it has to happen just to make ends meet, but we can perhaps be more mindful of the consequences of our actions. If we are doing it for our achievement or additional material comfort, we might not be preparing ourselves or our children for the future as well as we might. It can actually be a very self-focused attitude. We might think we are doing it for our family, but in reality it's for ourselves or we are teaching others that an achievement-orientation is a good thing.

It can help to think about the purpose of child*care* provision. If it's to develop ***our*** careers and buy material goods whilst emphasising greater levels of achievement-orientation with potential consequences of low self-esteem and ultimately feelings of failure, maybe it's not such a good thing. But if it's to teach children the joy of play and sharing, plus show them ways of relating to other human beings, then it's a very good thing indeed. It's all in the motivation and what we're trying to achieve by it.

An additional consequence of an achievement-orientation can be seen in society's current obesity and diabetes levels. We want to work hard to achieve and earn more, so we do not buy and prepare freshly cooked food because we want to spend our time doing other things. We are either working or spending time in leisure activities. So we buy pre-prepared food in packages or ready meals.

But think about this; how do you think the food is able to last on the shelf with such long sell-by dates? It's because of the chemicals that are necessary to pre-package it and the nature of the ingredients. The human body did not evolve to live on ready meals, it evolved as a result of freshly prepared food. It is not designed to survive on this type of fuel, so it has a reaction – obesity, diabetes and other illnesses. It rejects what we put into it. Not immediately (the body is a very resilient and hardy organism), but over time it will take a toll. It cannot continue to provide top performance if we don't put appropriate fuel into it. So our need to earn and achieve has a long-term effect on our health, making us upset and disappointed at what life has thrown at us. But it's not actually what life has thrown at us, it is an inevitable, logical consequence of our own choices and decisions.

Personality Types

There are numerous self-help tests and questionnaires that will highlight how 'well' you score on various personality attributes, such as openness, or whether you are more extraverted or introverted. Buddhist personality types put a completely different slant on it.

Buddhism outlines three broad types of dispositions called Aversive, Grasping and Deluded. Neither of these is better or worse than another, there is no 'right' type that we should strive for. We each have all three, but to differing degrees based on our circumstances, environments and predisposition. Knowing which type we are more predisposed towards can give us tremendous understanding in knowing why we are the way we are, and why we act and react in certain ways. By the same token, it helps us increase our understanding of others.

The 'Aversive' type is more likely to be grumbly and angry, perhaps bad-tempered. At its root, an Aversive type is upset at what is happening. The 'Grasping' type may say 'I'll be happy when' and sulk if they don't get what they want. At its root, a Grasping type has a future orientation, wanting things to always be better, whereas the Aversive type complains at how things currently are. A 'Deluded' type doesn't know what they want, so is less likely to be angry or future-focused. Instead, they might drift, perhaps caught up in the latest fashion or being prone to addictions and never 'achieving' anything in their life.

This demonstrates the negative aspects of each, but there are also positive aspects. The 'Grasper' holds the hopes and dreams for our future, as they look for ways to make the world a better place and what will make us happy. An Aversive will spot the injustices of the world, the unfairness of things, and speak up for the downtrodden and make change happen. Where the Grasper looks for what should be, the Aversive sees what's currently wrong. The Deluded type is likely to ask the really important questions. They will be the ones asking why we do things, when everyone else assumes it's the right way. They make life simpler and less complicated for everyone and can live in the moment joyfully and happily. Great art pieces are often produced by the Deluded types.

So which type are you? One way to find out is to look at how you react in everyday situations.

When driving, for example, the Grasper will be focused and disciplined, with the intention of getting to their destination as soon as possible. The Aversive will be angry at other drivers, perhaps exhibiting road-rage or experiencing stress in traffic jams. Not because they're late, but because they're being inconvenienced, whereas the Grasper may sulk at being held up. The Deluded type may drift between lanes and make decisions at the last minute when they realize what they should be doing. They might be less bothered in a traffic jam because they didn't really know what time they expected to arrive anyway.

Imagine you were visiting a friend and they'd just redecorated their apartment. The Grasper might talk about how it could be improved, perhaps by a painting here, or a display of plants there. An Aversive might spot all the things that are wrong and see how the colour scheme doesn't really match anything else. The Deluded might not even notice that things have changed but will notice the smell of paint and how the scent of flowers is trying to cover it up.

So how does this help us? Firstly, it gives us greater understanding into ourselves – it gives us a framework for why we do what we do and feel the way we feel. Now the reasons for our reactions can make sense. Secondly, it helps in our relationships with others through greater understanding of why they react the way they do.

Aversives and Graspers can often get on very well. Where the Aversive spots what's wrong, the Grasper can find the future solution. It creates a useful balance. The Aversive can also get on well with Deluded because the latter's easier temperament can have a calming influence. By the same token though, the indecision can be frustrating. Graspers and Deluded can also get on well, because of the dreaming, 'let's make the world a happier place' types of attitudes.

Where the problems often arise is with the same two personality types. Two Aversives can be a recipe for conflict. Two Graspers can lead to upset because of the conflicting dreams. Both parties are concentrating on the future, but unfortunately they have different visions of it. Two Deluded can be harmonious but mutually destructive because neither has the focus that might be needed to keep them on the straight and narrow or find a way forward.

For their own personal development, an Aversive might need to look at love and compassion to balance their judging and anger. A Grasper may need to practise more mindfulness so that they can focus more on the moment. A Deluded may need to look at wisdom and understanding in order to take a greater degree of personal responsibility.

The Mindful Path to Self-compassion by Dr Christopher Germer also outlines a set of personality types which can also help us understand more about ourselves. These aren't better or worse than the Buddhist personality types, they are just another tool to aid understanding and you will no doubt recognize similarities between them. Remember also that we are likely to have a disposition towards several and there is no 'right' type.

Caregiver – these types will immediately think of someone that needs help and support more than them. It's as if they want to sacrifice themselves for the good of others. Whilst this might sound very admirable, it can be dangerous because their own needs are often not met which can lead to subconscious feelings of anger and frustration which robs them of happiness. They are also prone to feelings of low self-worth and guilt, as they essentially consider everyone else's needs to be more important than their own.

Intellectual – this is where logic and rational thought are used to regulate or control emotions. An Intellectual also requires proof before something is believed. Many people in modern Western society have acquired this trait and it can account for the decline in religion and the increase in poor mental health through things such as depression and anxiety. Regulating emotions is explored further in Chapter 3 - Thoughts, Feeling and Emotions.

Perfectionists – striving to continually improve is not a bad thing, but the quest for perfection is very dangerous because it can never be achieved and it destroys happiness as nothing will ever be good enough.

Individualists – many of us have learnt, or strive for, independence and resilience. These are generally considered as 'good things'. Certainly its opposite, neediness, is an undesirable trait. Individualists don't expect help when they are in trouble and won't ask for it, but they also don't feel obligated to give it either. The trouble is that this independence is a complete illusion as we are all intricately tied up with each other and go through life both needing and giving support and help to others. It's what makes the world go round. So when an Individualist needs help, they will find it difficult to ask and the act of receiving it may destroy them mentally and emotionally.

Survivors – a Survivor feels that life has given them a rough deal and they often suffer from low self-esteem and diminished confidence. To a Survivor, the world feels very dark and harsh. A Survivor personality type does not need to have experienced major trauma or difficulties, it's more about having a negative, harsh view of the world regardless of what's happened. Even good things happening to a Survivor will create negative feelings – they may not spot that it has even happened, or expect they'll lose it or may feel unjustified in having it.

Workhorse – this is the person who is dominated by an achievement orientation. It's all about getting the job done, working hard and achieving. This personality type is often required to achieve a high position in a chosen career or sporting success and is a greatly valued trait in Western society. Unfortunately though, a Workhorse will often miss out on the simple pleasures to be found all around us and can never rest or be satisfied, as there's always something else to do, something else to be achieved. A major risk for a

Workhorse is that their children will grow up but they feel as though they have missed out on it. They also have increased risks of stress and lifestyle-related illnesses such as heart disease, diabetes, cancer and stroke.

Butterfly – full of spontaneity and pleasure-seeking, the Butterfly can be a joy to be around. But unfortunately, the Butterfly never settles so this personality type never achieves mastery of anything and drifts from interest to new interest, perhaps never developing a career or settling into a long-term loving relationship. They are also at risk of addictions and being tempted into dangerous lifestyles because of their lack of focus and discipline.

Outsider – these people never quite fit into mainstream society, perhaps due to race, sexual orientation, religion, lifestyle preferences or a million and one other things that make them 'different'. But it is these differences that lead to creativity and many artists and other geniuses, such as Einstein, would clearly fit into this personality type. An Outsider can suffer from alienation unless they find a group of other like-minded individuals, but the cause of the 'difference' can then contribute to an unhelpful self-identity. In effect, they relate more to their point of differentiation than to their common humanity, thus increasing the degree of separation, discrimination and victimisation they feel.

Moralist – this means having a rigid sense of

right and wrong, with clear rules of conduct and behaviour required of others. A Moralist will thrive in official and authoritarian roles such as law enforcement or the civil service, but may struggle with life's natural shades of grey.

There are many other categories of personality types, such as the Jungian Archetypes or those explained by Caroline Myss in her writings. The trick with all of them is to identify those aspects useful in developing understanding, rather than becoming attached to a label or particular type and then using it to drive your life or justify attitudes. For example, a Moralist could use their personality type to help explain why they often struggle to understand why people act in certain ways. A Workhorse might see why they get upset with their son's apparent lack of drive and ambition – perhaps it's because they are a Butterfly, rather than a 'waster' or unambitious.

Areas for Contemplation

♦ When a problem arises, which of these two are you more likely to ask; "what happened?", or "who's fault is it?".

♦ Are you quick to judgement?

♦ Can you remember an occasion when you came to the wrong conclusion? Did you accept your error gracefully or defend why you came to that conclusion?

♦ How far do you blame other people, circumstances or events for what has happened in your life?

♦ Where have your opportunities in life come from – your hard work and perseverance or lucky breaks?

♦ Have you ever been in the right place at the right time? Would other people agree with that conclusion?

♦ Has anyone ever said that you take things too personally?

♦ Which of the three Buddhist personality types do you feel most accurately reflects you – Aversive, Grasping or Deluded? Why? Has it ever caused you problems? What happened?

♦ Do you feel any of the other personality types describes you? Which areas of your life and attitudes does it help to explain?

♦ Can you see any of the personality types in people you know? How might it change how you relate to them?

Chapter 3

Thoughts, Feelings and Emotions

It is important to understand thoughts, feelings and emotions as the three together ultimately govern our actions and reactions.

Thoughts are the endless things that go on in our conscious mind. For many of us, that will be a stream of continuous chatter in our head. Others experience it more visually as they think in pictures and images but the effect is the same – an endless stream of stuff going on in our mind.

Feelings are whether we perceive something as positive, negative or neutral. Something makes us feel happy so that gives us a positive feeling, whereas something that makes us angry creates a negative feeling. Most of the things we encounter are neutral and generate indifference or unawareness.

Emotions are more deep-seated and we tend to feel them within our bodies, rather than think them in our minds. Our body feels a certain way when we are angry, perhaps rigid or tight, but when we are happy we feel lighter and looser. Anxiety may lead to a tightness or fluttering in the stomach – 'butterflies'. However, unless we are in tune with our emotions and bodily sensations, we won't be aware of this and may put it down to a health issue.

We tend to think that thoughts come first and these lead to feelings and emotions, but that's not the correct sequence. We have the feeling first, i.e. a positive or negative reaction to something, which then creates an emotion within us which then leads to a conscious thought about it. An action may then arise from the thought, as a result of it. It is technically possible for actions to arise directly from emotions but it's usually the case that we are unaware of the intervening thought, rather than it not actually happening.

Feelings and emotions arise through our upbringing and our nature. They are very deep-seated and are often subconscious reactions to an event, based on previous patterns. Back when we were cave dwellers we might see a tiger's tail, for instance, which created an emotional subconscious reaction of fear. This reaction then leads to the thought; 'it's a tiger, what will I do?' Remember though that we didn't actually see the tiger, we saw a tail, then made the connection. The connection may or may not have been accurate, but the emotion and therefore the thought is still there. This emotion is a good thing though, because it might be a tiger and we might have to take action. Our emotions are there for a reason; to protect and inform us. Without the emotion we might see the tail but not generate the thought 'it's a tiger' and so do nothing, meaning we might have been eaten.

We are often taught to suppress our emotions.

Tears are a physical output of an emotion but many of us are taught to not cry, which creates the reaction of 'emotions are bad, I better not have them'. The example of 'stiff upper lip' or 'we need to be strong' are other instances of how we are taught to suppress our emotions, or to get over them. But they are real and they are there. The act of suppressing them means we switch off from our natural humanity and lose a vital component of how to live. Suppressed emotions don't go away, they lie dormant but will come out at some point when we are less able to control them. It's a bit like sending them down to the basement where they can build up their strength, unnoticed. They don't go anywhere, they just get stronger until one day they burst out to our detriment.

So rather than suppressing them, we need to realize them and see what they are telling us. This doesn't necessarily mean we have public demonstrations of emotions, that might not be appropriate in our society or culture, although it is in some. Instead we can get in touch with them and realize what they are telling us. They are there to inform and guide us and we can use them as such.

Emotions make useful servants but terrible masters. This concept is demonstrated by an example adapted from *The Road Less Travelled* by M. Scott Peck. In his book he uses the analogy of a slave plantation owner to demonstrate the effect of emotions, but in this adaptation I've chosen a factory owner where the workers represent emotions.

If the workers feel oppressed or that their views are not taken into account, they will be less motivated and not willing to work for the owner. They might put up with the management style for a while but eventually they may leave or their productivity will drop, creating a damaging effect on the business, possibly leading to failure and bankruptcy. The opposite approach is to give the workers complete freedom but in this event the owner might come in one day and find out that no one has turned up for work and all his stock and machinery have been stolen and sold.

The other alternative is to take a balanced approach where the owner understands the concerns of the workers and listens to them, taking action where appropriate to increase motivation and enthusiasm for the work. The owner may also identify those workers who have particular strengths that can be used for everyone's benefit and increased happiness, or areas that aren't working well and respond appropriately. This is more likely to lead to longer term success for the business and more happiness all round.

In our lives, if we suppress our emotions we are like the first owner and will ultimately suffer as a result. If we are like the second approach we may eventually become an emotional wreck as we are controlled by them and find it difficult to function. The third route is where we are aware of our emotions and the consequences of them so that we can work with them for our greater benefit.

Another useful analogy for why it is helpful to try and get more in tune with our emotions is that without them we are trying to live with one arm tied behind our back, which has a very detrimental 'double whammy' effect. First of all, emotions are a key facet of our basic humanity and without them we would be dead. So trying to live without them or controlling them means that we are missing out on an incredibly valuable tool to help us with our lives. Secondly, if you've ever tried doing anything with only one hand you'll realize that it's really hard to do and you're more likely to make mistakes, take longer and get frustrated. So we both miss out on an incredibly useful tool and make life harder for ourselves.

Identifying an emotional reaction is also a key component of anger management. We might believe that anger is a thought, but before it happens there will be a reaction within the body. There are analogies to describe this reaction – our hackles are raised, our blood is boiling, we see red. These are all tangible descriptions of the emotion and feeling that we can relate to. The trick with anger management is to spot these feelings before they lead to thoughts. We feel the reaction and it indicates to us that we are getting angry. It doesn't tell us what we're angry about, only that anger is arising but we can use this knowledge, this feeling, to watch our thoughts and the subsequent actions. With practise we can learn to spot these feelings before they become too strong. We can then work with them, so that our thoughts and actions become less anger-driven.

This principle works with many other things that we call 'feelings'. I can tell when I'm becoming anxious because I feel a tightening in the belly (butterflies in the stomach), my heart beats faster and I find myself fidgeting and wringing my hands. When I spot these things happening I realize that I am feeling anxious and can act accordingly. When I'm feeling low or depressed my shoulders sink and I find myself sighing a lot.

We can use the mindfulness techniques highlighted in Chapter 11 - Regular Practises and Activities to help us identify the emotions we have, so that over time we build a better picture of the type of person we are, identifying both strengths and areas that we might want to work on.

Thinking Patterns

I'm greatly indebted to Cognitive-Behavioural Therapy (CBT) for the help it gave me in reducing my anxiety. The principles below are from CBT and they illustrate ways of thinking that explain why we see the world the way we do and why we feel as we do.

Black and white thinking. This means seeing the world in a certain way without allowing for any shades of grey. It's tempting to have a framework for the way the world works that we can latch on to, a set of rules, if you like. Unfortunately, they don't exist. For every crime you can mention, it's possible to imagine an occasion when it might actually be acceptable, or at least understandable.

Take murder, for example. Would it be wrong to assassinate a leader who kills and brutalises his people? Is killing this one person not sometimes more favourable than allowing the deaths of thousands of innocent people? Would an assassination of Hitler not have saved millions of lives and unprecedented levels of destruction? If we had bombed Auschwitz and the other death camps, could millions of lives not have been saved?

On the other hand, removing brutal dictatorships or regimes can often unleash the gates of hell for the people of the country. We saw this in Yugoslavia, Afghanistan (after the end of the Russian occupation) and Iraq. So it's never simple, and this lack of simplicity is the main problem with black and white thinking. Nothing is ever as simple and clear cut as we would like it to be.

We can see black and white thinking with phrases such as 'you're either with us or against us'. Perhaps, I'm neither, maybe I just see it differently and wonder if there might be other alternatives to explore. Another example is people saying 'obviously' when explaining a situation. Perhaps there are other explanations meaning that, by definition, the answer isn't completely obvious and might actually be a bit more grey.

Over-generalization. We can recognize this when people say 'why does this always happen to me?'. It doesn't always happen. It might **usually** or **often** happen (especially if we repeat patterns of past behaviour), but it won't **always** happen. This is a close cousin of black and white thinking because it doesn't leave room for the natural shades of grey that the world is. Times and attitudes change, so nothing can ever be 'always'.

All or nothing. This is another close cousin of black and white thinking and is clearly seen with perfectionists. Unless things are perfect, they are wrong or not good enough. Striving for better and more all the time is like an achievement orientation in that we will never be satisfied. Having perfectionist tendencies means that we have, in effect, decided that we can never be happy because something will always need to be improved or made better.

An example would be two people returning from holiday who had to wait for a taxi at the airport longer than planned, then got stuck in a traffic jam and ended up having a row. When asked how the holiday went they might say that the journey home ruined it. The last hour of a two week holiday cannot 'ruin' an entire fortnight. The taxi home cannot have had an impact on anything that went before it but because that one element at the end was unpleasant, the whole thing was 'ruined'.

There is no 'perfect', other than how we define it ourselves. Ask two people what 'perfect' is and they will give two answers, so our definition is personal. So seeking perfection means we are continually battling ourselves, rather than taking pleasure in what we have. Good enough usually is good enough.

Catastrophizing. This happens when people assume that the worst possible outcome will happen. We have a pain in our chest and assume it must be the start of heart disease or cancer. Our cold becomes a serious infection or the start of bronchitis when in reality it's just a few days of inconvenience.

The exact opposite of this, unbridled optimism, can also be an issue. It can be very endearing when someone always sees the best in a situation or is always looking positively at something, but if it is not accompanied by wisdom it can create equally as many problems. The partner who feels their love can transform a violent or abusive partner is suffering from this because they don't appreciate the full extent of the damage inflicted on them and their family, so don't pursue other courses of action, such as leaving.

Unbridled optimism is sometimes called a

'Pollyanna syndrome' after the character in a children's book by Eleanor H Porter. Pollyanna was a child who lived in a harsh and brutal environment and her defense mechanism was to always see the best in a situation, so that she didn't become overwhelmed and depressed at what was happening. The ultimate outcome of this was when she lost the use of a leg and was glad as it would help her in a hopping contest.

Taking it Personally. Much to the disgust of our ego, it's not always about us. Most people are so caught up in their own lives that they don't notice what's going on around them. So when they don't say 'hello' in the street or appear to snub you, it's often got nothing at all to do with you and everything to do with them. If we take it as a personal affront we might lose friends when in reality they might be suffering and really need our help, but we're so caught up in our own pride that we fail to notice. When they can't make it to events we think they don't like us anymore when in reality they might have problems at home and really need a friend, but their own pride prevents them from asking. So rather than helping someone who desperately needs our support, we sulk and condemn them.

Controlling. This is actually at the root of many of our problems and isn't solely related to our thinking patterns. We try to control the people and events in the world around us and expect that we can. We then get upset because things don't go the way they 'should' or someone didn't do what you felt they 'should' do. We can call this the 'tyranny of the should' because we have fixed views on the way things should be, then try to make it that way. But things won't go the way we think they should, they'll go the way they are going to go, regardless of how we think they should go.

The real problem here is one of expectation. We expect things to happen in a certain way then get upset when they don't. The problem isn't necessarily what's actually happened, it's that we expected or hoped something different would happen. If we didn't have the expectation, we wouldn't be upset at how things actually went.

You may hear people say things such as 'the dog has a mind of its own', or a partner 'won't do as he's told'. Yes, the dog does have a mind of its own, it's called 'personality'. No, he won't do as he's told – why should he? As a grown adult with a mind of his own he can make his own decisions, which may or may not be what you want. But this isn't really the problem, the problem is that we expect something different. If we stop having expectations then we can appreciate them for who and what they are, rather than what they can do for us.

Comparing. As human beings we need some kind of reference point to give us a sense of where we are in the world. For example, we know we are adult because of the opposite reference point – being a child. We know we are tall because of the opposite reference point – short. As mentioned in the 'Separation, Discrimination and Perception' section in Chapter 1, we live in a world of opposites, of duality. Reference points only become an issue if inappropriate references are used. So if we compare ourselves to our rich, beautiful, intelligent sister we feel depressed. But if we compare ourselves to the same sister but view her as jealous, competitive, self-obsessed and not caring of her family, we may have a completely different interpretation.

Be very, very careful about who you compare yourself to. In our celebrity, achievement-oriented culture it's always possible to find someone we perceive as 'better' than us, but all this does is make us feel inferior. This is where your role models and who you aspire to be are important. If you compare yourself to what you were and see progress, that's a good thing. If you compare yourself to someone else, that's dangerous, discriminatory and judging, so not helpful.

Irrational beliefs. The early proponents of CBT believed that our problems were due to our irrational beliefs. The therapeutic challenge, then, was to identify which irrational beliefs were held and counter them. Example of the types of beliefs we may hold are:

♦ I need to be loved and approved of by everyone.

♦ In order to be a worthwhile person, I need to be good at everything.

♦ Bad people, including myself, need to be punished.

♦ If things are not the way I want them to be, it's a disaster.

♦ I have no real control over my problems as they are caused by external factors.

♦ Reminding myself of the awful things that can happen makes them less likely to happen.

♦ It's easier to avoid problems than to face them and take responsibility.

♦ I need someone to take care of me.

♦ I can't change my behaviour because it's in my genes or a result of my past.

♦ I am responsible for fixing other people's problems.

(Adapted from Ellis, 1962 and cited in Hough, 2010)

The interesting thing about several items on this list is that we will often refuse to acknowledge that we think this way, at least in public. But deep down many of us **do** think in one or more of these ways and it causes enormous problems.

This is where therapy is useful because it can help us to realize which irrational beliefs we hold, then do something about them. A skilled therapist can help us to identify how we think and the consequences, but won't tell us what's 'wrong'. The reason for this is that when we realize for ourselves what we're doing, we internalize it and make it ours. Because it's ours we're motivated to try and change it, rather than responding to what someone else has told us to do.

It also helps to know the strength and depth of our feelings, emotions and thinking patterns. Sometimes, knowledge of a way of thinking is enough in itself to change the way we act and respond. We have learnt to act in a certain way as a result of our upbringing and experiences, so it feels 'normal' to us. But sometimes simply knowing the consequences of a way of thinking and acting can be enough to change it.

There will be other emotions or thinking patterns we have that are much more deep-seated. They feel like a core part of us and we really can't see any other way of acting. An analogy for this would be like trying to explain to a fish what water was. If the fish could talk it wouldn't understand what water is because it doesn't know anything else. But if it experienced being out of the water it would realize the difference and would want to go back as soon as it could to where it's comfortable and what it knows about. This is why asking someone to act in a different way can be like asking them to cut their arm off. Ways of acting can be like addictions and the very thought of doing something different or giving something up sends us into a spiral of fear or anger.

Opinions

Highly-opinionated people have a tendency to spend their lives inadvertently annoying and upsetting others. It is understandable that idealistic people (often the young) want to change the world and perhaps it is right that they try to do so. But the risk is that in making our mark on the world or attempting to get respect or disguise our low self-esteem, we don't listen and instead try to foist our opinion on others. This is what annoys people and prevents the growth of true wisdom and knowledge.

When Westerners see people from the East or Muslims bend down to 'kiss the ground', we are missing the point. They are actually prostrating to develop respect and humility. There was a good example when the Pakistan cricket team toured England. Whenever a Pakistani batsman reached a significant milestone, such as scoring 50 or 100 runs, they would bend down and kiss the ground, or at least that's how it was reported by the commentators. What they were actually doing was prostrating to Allah. They were thanking Allah for granting them the good fortune to achieve such a high score and dedicating it to his glory. It also shows how we can completely miss the point of something if we approach it with our own prejudices and opinions, rather than considering it from the perspective of the person doing it.

The world is evolving as it will, for better or worse, taking us along with it. We look at society around us and conform to what we think is 'right', condemning those we think are 'wrong'. We then try to make those we think are 'wrong' conform to our way of thinking. After all, we're right. Except we only think we're right if we are conforming to *our* society's values - and they are continually changing. And other societies, such as France or the USA or Afghanistan, have different values and views of what's 'right'.

Remember also that it's not so long ago that the USA, the 'land of the free', fought a civil war with the right to use slaves as a major contributory factor to its cause. This same slavery was developed, run and funded by the British and other European nations. We might find it abhorrent now, but only 200 years ago it felt perfectly normal to take people forcibly from their homes and ship them 3,000 miles away – shackled in irons - to make them grow tobacco and cotton to make us wealthier. It's only recently that the last veteran of WW1 died. The 'Great War', where we thought it was a good idea to kill millions of European youths for the pride of royal families and the right to enslave and 'civilise' Africa.

But being opinionated doesn't just apply to concepts such as politics or our view of nations and religions, it applies equally well to individuals. Following the sequence of separation and discrimination, judgement and control, we will often find ourselves judging others, or forming an opinion of them. But if we find out more about the person and their history, the reasons why they act the way they do may become very apparent and lead to compassion and understanding, rather than forming a negative opinion.

I know someone who is very rigid in their thinking and ways of approaching the world. Everything has to be on time and she will often arrive too early for events and have to wait around for a while. I remember talking to her about her schooldays and she told me how the bus left at a very precise time to take the pupils home and that they had to walk a specific path through the grounds to get to it. There was only just enough time after the end of classes to make it and any diversion from the normal route would mean being late for the bus. There wasn't a later bus. So deviations from the fixed path would cause enormous stress.

The school also had very precise rules about uniforms and exactly how they were to be worn. So if a tie was slightly to the side, for example, it would lead to punishments such as detention. Running for the bus via a slightly different route whilst holding on to clothes to keep them precise became a major trauma. No wonder she is very uptight and rigid about the way things have to be. I used to feel real annoyance at her rigidity and rules, but now I feel only compassion as I know exactly where it came from and can see the pain and difficulties caused by it.

A more extreme example came from a previous colleague who was very angry and opinionated. There was a right way to do things and he knew what it was. There was no compromise and the tone of communications was usually very harsh and condemnatory. He was not a pleasant person to work alongside in a team. I once heard the phrase; "when the mouth speaks poison, the heart is full of pain" so I reached out to him as I was interested in his history and what caused the pain.

When he was a child of around 10 years old, the family was made destitute and homeless but he continued to go to school throughout and gained a postgraduate degree before building a successful career. But he never forgot the shame and humiliation of childhood. When something appeared to threaten his position he reacted by lashing out to demonstrate how good he was at the job and how he must, therefore, be right. Deep down, he felt that a challenge to his opinion was a challenge to his status, and that brought back all the childhood fears of humiliation followed by the determination to never allow anything like it to happen again. Now I could see where the pain, and thus the poison, came from. He never did change his working style, but I found him much less abrasive from that point onwards because I knew not to take it personally as it was his childhood trauma speaking.

Be careful of getting caught up in 'rights' and 'wrongs'. Everyone has different views and opinions, some of them helpful and others less so, but all of them merely a product of their society and environment, and all ultimately leading to suffering and problems for them.

Attitudes and Delusions

Attitudes are states of mind. Helpful, useful ones can be called virtuous, whereas negative, unhelpful ones can be called delusions. They're called delusions because we think they're normal, but this is deluded because what's 'normal' about filling your mind with stuff that stresses or displeases you? Remember too that these attitudes are all internal. They do not come from outside, we created them all by ourselves, although usually subconsciously and generally to fit in with family, friends, society, etc.

Many of these states of mind are discussed in modern psychology, self-help and therapy. The aim should be to identify the delusions and try to remove them, whilst developing more virtuous attitudes instead. Delusions are things such as anger, hatred, bitterness, jealousy, pride, etc. Virtuous states of mind include love, compassion, patience, caring, tolerance and wisdom.

A traditional tale from the Cherokee Nation of American First Peoples demonstrates the difference between virtuous and delusional states of mind. An old grandfather is talking to his grandson one day, telling him a tale of two wolves that live inside us, constantly at war with each other. One wolf, he says, represents love, compassion and kindness. The other represents anger, bitterness and hatred. The boy contemplates this for a moment before asking which one wins. 'The one you feed most', replies the grandfather.

Self-focus

Self-focus is the ultimate personal delusion we have. It is the source from which all others flow and we all have it to a greater or lesser degree. A strong sense of self is what causes our problems. By reducing it, we become happier plus more peaceful and joyful.

We've all encountered the person who thinks only of themselves and not of others, who thinks everything is about them. They assume their view of the world is right and that anyone who doesn't agree with them is either out to get them or needs 'sorting out'. It's very hard to discuss things with someone like that because they get angry, frustrated and upset when you don't conform to their way of thinking – the way you 'should' think. The language they use is filled with phrases such as '*everyone is…*', because they can't see that not everyone thinks the way they do and that they're not the centre of the universe. Or they might claim that they are just trying to make things right. They're actually trying to impose their own personal opinion and view of the world on others.

For someone with a strong sense of self-focus, putting themselves in someone else's shoes is a lost concept. They might talk about caring or generosity for a short while, but it will eventually come back to what **they** expect to get out of it, such as gratitude.

There are some very long complicated arguments from philosophy, psychology and religion about definitions of the 'self', but I think of it as an ego-driven nature which focuses on ourselves all the time. In any situation it looks at what it thinks is best for us, but only from our perspective. If something happens, it looks at the effect on ourselves, rather than the wider picture.

As an example, think of what happened the last time you walked past a homeless person or there was someone who seemed a bit strange at the bus stop. What did you do? Did you hope they wouldn't get on your bus and sit next to you? Did you walk straight past the homeless person, hoping they didn't catch your eye, as you might feel the need to give them something but they'd '*only spend it on drink or drugs*'?

This is the self, or ego-driven nature, at work. It's there when we feel anxious, depressed, jealous, bitter or any of the other negative feelings we have. It's not a particularly happy place to spend our lives.

Self-focus is 'the big one' and is where all our other issues come from. We all have a life-story to tell - the homeless person wasn't born the way you currently see them. They might have been struggling all their life following abuse as a child and then, despite their best efforts, lost their home through no fault of their own. The strange person at the bus stop might be someone's mother who is suffering from dementia and has walked away from the nursing home. She now needs someone to look after her until the emergency services arrive to take her back to her loving family who miss her terribly and worry about her endlessly.

Society tells us to 'look after number one', but in reality this just causes problems. How do you feel when you've received another boring jumper at Christmas, or a present that quite clearly didn't take your needs into account or demonstrates a lack of understanding about what you like? Now imagine that you've put thought into buying the perfect present for someone and you see their face light up with joy when receiving it, especially if they didn't expect it. Or think of the joy we often see on someone's face when we help them out or give them a present, something that *they* truly want and can appreciate. It brings pleasure to everyone, including a nice rosy glow inside ourselves.

This is when we are thinking of other people, rather than ourselves.

Which situation makes you feel happiest? Receiving the Christmas jumper or the joy of giving? In the first situation, you're thinking about yourself and what you're getting out of it rather than the giver's motivation. In the second, you get enormous pleasure from doing something for someone else.

Self-focus is the former and leads only to unhappiness. As you make your way through life you will see countless examples of self-focus, both in you and others. Psychology has a name for excessive self-focus - narcissism. But it's nothing new, it's been around for millennia.

Our world as we see it is determined by our self-focus. Being able to reduce the usual self-focused approach allows us to see everything free from prejudices, opinions and perceptions. Living in our self-focused, ego-driven nature means we often miss the good things and see only the negative. We don't generate understanding of what's really going on so can't make effective judgements. Reducing our self-focus means reducing the ego and starting to think of others more. You might even think of it as compassion and wisdom.

Anger, Bitterness and Jealousy

People consumed with rage are not beautiful

or pretty. Instead, they are scary, ugly and capable of inflicting great harm on themselves and others. It's a very unpleasant feeling which can last for decades and tear families apart. Even in the short-term, it deprives you of your happiness and peace of mind. You can't be angry plus happy and peaceful at the same time. You can only be one or the other.

So why do we do it? Self-focus, basically. We're concentrating so much on ourselves and our own needs that we fail to take anyone else into account, or we don't consider our inability to change a situation. We get frustrated because we can't make the world the way we think it should be, or want other people to stop annoying us. So it's all about us. Can you imagine being angry whilst giving a gift, lovingly chosen, for someone? It can't happen. Focusing on other people rather than ourselves destroys anger but self-focus fuels it.

Let's look at an example. Imagine that someone cuts you up at a roundabout. We might get angry and furious, how dare they charge in front – they should wait their turn !!! Well, perhaps that person is actually on their way to a hospital because they've just been told their dad has had a heart attack and might die any minute. If you knew that, would you have willingly let them in? Probably. So thinking about yourself led to anger, but considering others dissolved it.

Perhaps the person wasn't on their way to the

hospital, maybe they were just an arrogant bully who thought they deserved the space because of who they think they are and their sense of entitlement. Did your anger change them? No. What effect did it have? It made you very unappealing – ugly, scary and red in the face with no peace or happiness. And for what benefit did you get into that horrible state of mind? Your actions did not change the situation or the arrogant bully one bit. In fact, he probably didn't even notice, or might actually have enjoyed winding you up. He won, you're angry, upset and have lost. Next time, give him a cheery wave and a big smile, that'll throw him - and you'll stay happy and peaceful.

Another question to ask is whether something is worth destroying your peace and happiness over, in order to prove yourself right. Anger makes you ugly and bitter, whereas happiness and peace feel nice. The desire to be right and prove it often comes from pride, which is another form of self-focus. But if it leads to anger - and therefore makes you ugly, unattractive and unhappy, what's the point? If it doesn't change the other person's actions or behaviour and only makes you unhappy, why bother?

Attachment

This can be a difficult one to grasp at first. Essentially, it says that the cause of suffering is being attached to something. Because everything (including us) eventually decays and dies, we're setting ourselves up to suffer feelings of loss for the rest of our lives. We spend our lives desiring, wanting and aiming for things, only to find the following:

- It doesn't live up to expectations (perhaps that new job with more money limits your free time or is too stressful, or the holiday is disappointing)

- The novelty wears off (the new car or partner is great for 12-18 months or so, then you want a change)

- The price is too high (you can no longer afford your home because circumstances have changed, such as a marriage break-up or losing your job)

- It causes you problems (the unreliable car, or the child that grows up to be an alcoholic drug user or a disappointment in other ways, after your high hopes for them)

- It loses its value to you or it breaks (your home gets broken into so that it no longer feels like a safe haven or you crash the car).

When we're talking about ourselves and our loved ones we can also add in that they get sick, old and die, but not necessarily in that order.

So we spend our lives chasing things that are ultimately going to disappoint us when one or more of the above things happen. The car, house, job, money, partner, children, etc. will not make us permanently happy as ultimately they may disappoint us, let us down, we lose them, or they become a burden on us. That's not to say they can't give us pleasure - they can - but not long-term, permanent, stable peace and happiness. We have to find that from somewhere else, rather than expecting these external things to provide it for us.

The place it comes from is within ourselves. We need to find our own means of being content *regardless of what we encounter or have.* Then the external objects we so desire can become *extra sources* of pleasure and joy to *increase* our happiness, rather than expecting them to be the *cause* of it. And when we lose them or they no longer provide the pleasure they used to, we don't get unhappy because our happiness wasn't dependent on them. Then we can love and treasure them every moment whilst we have them because of the joy they give us, rather than being dependent on them and ultimately suffering when they're gone or no longer meeting expectations.

This leads to an acceptance of the way the world is, rather than a continual focus on changing it. The world around us is continually changing and evolving anyway, with people and events coming into our world, affecting us, and then leaving it again. Continually and non-stop — and there's nothing we can do about it. We can alter our circumstances to make things more comfortable and pleasurable as much as we like, but ultimately it will change beyond our control.

The real cause of our suffering is not that the world is continually changing and evolving, it's that we expect it to stay the same and conform to our wishes. That's never going to happen. But if we accept that everything we desire will ultimately upset us or we'll lose it, then our attitude to the world will be totally different. We wouldn't put all our time and energy into chasing external achievements. Instead we could take pleasure in what's around us and what we have, then let it go when its time has come to depart (whatever or whomever 'it' is), knowing that our lives were more joyful and richer for the time we had with it.

As The Serenity Prayer from Christianity says; "*Lord, grant me the courage to change the things I can, the strength to cope with the things I can't, and the wisdom to know the difference.*"

Levels of Attachment

The writer don Miguel Ruiz Jr. describes the depths of attachment we feel towards different things in his beautiful little book, *The Five levels of Attachment.*

Using the analogy of a sporting event such as a football game, we can identify how strongly attached we are to a particular object, person or concept by reviewing which of the five levels below feel most appropriate.

At Level 1 we might come across a football game or other event and watch it because we enjoy it. We might become immersed in watching the action flow back and forth but have no particular interest in either of the teams or what the final result is. When the game is over we simply walk away, applauding both teams gratefully and warmly for the pleasure given.

Level 2 is similar to Level 1 but now we start to form preferences towards one side or the other. It's not a big deal though and it doesn't really matter to us who wins, but maybe one side is the underdog or plays in a way that we feel drawn towards or like the look of, so we would prefer them to win. When the game is over we walk away having enjoyed the match but not unduly concerned whether the team for whom we had a preference actually won or not.

Level 3 follows from Level 2 but now we are actively interested in one side or another. We support one side and want them to win. It's not a crisis if they lose, but we definitely feel a bit disappointed if they do. Level 3 also allows us to associate with other people who follow the same team as we have something in common with which to forge an identity and relationships. We can also share a common bond with other people who enjoy the sport but who follow a different team.

A Level 4 attachment indicates an avid supporter. As well as going to games whenever they can, it will be a big part of their conversation and when they come into work on a Monday morning their colleagues can tell by their demeanour whether their preferred team won or lost.

Level 5 would demonstrate total commitment, a true fanatic. They would be prepared to follow their team around the world regardless of the expense and it will influence their communication and daily interactions to a large degree. Non-supporters would be treated with distrust or disdain and ultimately they may even risk going to prison or physical harm for their loyalty or commitment.

All of us exhibit different levels of attachment to the environment around us. We may have a Level 5 attachment to our family and children where we really would be willing to lay down our lives for them, whereas our job may be a Level 2. We may also find that our attachment level changes over time. Someone who is young, ambitious and money-driven may have a Level 4 or 5 attachment to income and career, but after middle-age it might change to a 2 as other things take priority. We also tend to have a predominant overall level, so we might view life as a 4 or 5 so take things very seriously, or be at 2 so are very easy-going and laid back.

The greater the degree of attachment to something, the more we run the risk of unhappiness when it lets us down or stops meeting our expectations. Our happiness becomes intimately tied up with it, meaning that we give our ability to be happy over to whatever it is. In effect, we sacrifice our own personal power to the object of attachment. Because we separate, discriminate, judge and control, most of us go through life at Level 3 and 4, although for some things it will be at 5 (such as our children). True happiness and peace comes from Levels 1 and 2 as we don't get attached to anything so can enjoy everything for what it truly is, rather than what it does for us.

A stronger degree of attachment can also lead to an inability to see a situation clearly. Don Miguel Ruiz Jr. explains how the levels can be likened to windows or mirrors of different quality. At Level 1 there is, in effect, no mirror as we see directly into what's happening without being fooled by anything, like a clear window. At Level 2 we see our reflection coming back at us and start to form judgements based on what we see. At Level 3 our preferences start to distort the reflection we see. It's as if we are looking at a fairground mirror that artificially makes us look fat or thin or bent to a strange angle. We know it's us but we look distorted as we're not seeing clearly. We're not really that shape, but we do feel as if we are because of what we're looking at and how we interpret it.

Level 4 is called the smoky mirror as it's difficult to see anything in it at all, other than distorted, inaccurate patterns. Level 5 is like a brick wall. We don't get any reflection back with which to form a picture, it's all very solid and rigid and we only see things one way with no alternatives at all.

We can identify our level of attachment to anything by considering the depth of our desire to be with it, or what our reaction would be if we were to lose it. If we would consider the loss as a major trauma then it is a high attachment, such as a 4 or 5. But if we can get pleasure without attachment, i.e. not suffering so much if we lost it or it created an inconvenience for us, then it is more likely to be closer to 2. The more items and concepts we identify at levels 3 to 5, the more we will suffer generally from attachment and an inability to see the world clearly.

Areas for Contemplation

- ♦ What are your predominant thoughts, feelings and emotions? Look back over your past and see if you can identify where they came from and why they have such importance for you.

- ♦ Which of your thoughts, feelings and emotions are helpful for you, and which aren't?

- ♦ Can you sense where different emotions are felt in your body? Is there anything which increases or reduces the sensation?

♦ What have other people said are your predominant thoughts, feelings and emotions? Are they right? If they aren't right, where did they get the impression from and is it justified?

♦ How in tune with your emotions are you? Do you suppress them or are you comfortable expressing them? Have either of these two approaches helped or harmed you and in what circumstances?

♦ What emotions or reactions in others create an effect in you? Why? Do you consider this response helpful or not? Why?

♦ What specific thinking patterns do you exhibit and in what circumstances? Has it ever caused you a problem?

♦ Would you consider yourself to be opinionated or do you prefer to keep your views to yourself? Would others agree?

♦ Can you remember any instances when you acted under self-focus to the detriment of yourself or others? What was the outcome?

♦ What areas of your life do you feel most attached to? To what level of attachment?

Chapter 4

Our Relationship with the World

Psychologists and scientists often discuss whether we become the way we are (nurture) or if we are born like that, with all our traits and ways of being (nature). It's as if it needs to be one or the other. It could, of course, be a bit of each or even something else entirely.

In addition to nature or nurture, we could also introduce our life circumstances and immediate mood. We might be born with a tendency towards anger but are brought up in a loving, caring environment so that when things are going generally well for us, we feel okay. If our car was broken into we'd be able to deal with it without getting too upset or angry. But if we're having a bad day then the anger reaction may surface. If you were to conduct surveys on levels of happiness and contentment then we might score a 7 out of 10. But if we're feeling good on the day we were asked, we might score an 8. On the other hand, if our car had just been broken into, we might give a 5 or 6.

So rather than simply nature or nurture, we could give a weighting to each of the four factors. We could give 30% each to nature, nurture and circumstances, with 10% allocated to how we feel at that moment. This would mean that 70% of how we feel is not down to our nature, it is down to us and we can take personal responsibility for it. We can't change our upbringing, but we can see how it has affected us and we can work towards making our circumstances more comfortable for ourselves. Not by trying to control what happens, but by knowing what makes us tick and what our true passions are, then moving more towards them.

This split also accounts for why we tend to revert to our usual way of relating to the world after a significant change. So if we win the lottery but were generally miserable beforehand, then after around 18-24 months we will be miserable again. Wealthier perhaps, but not really much happier. 60% of our happiness feelings come from nature and nurture, but only 30% from our circumstances – wealth, in the case of a lottery win. After the novelty has worn off, the immediate mood reverts to our more natural way of being, so we lose the short-term boost of happiness the win gave us.

The same also works in reverse. If we experience a major trauma such as being made disabled our natural state will normally return, e.g. to a general feeling of happiness and contentment when we have adjusted to the new circumstances of our life and accepted it as a 'new normal'.

The 'Okay' Feeling

The writer Jeff Foster gives a good explanation of how this process of nurturing, circumstances and immediate environment combines to determine how we feel. When we are in the womb we feel safe and comfortable with all our needs looked after, without us having to ask. It just happens. This is also where our nature is formed. Then, the moment we are born, this feeling of safety and security is removed. We change from a feeling of okay to 'not-okay'. We don't know where we are or what has happened so we respond in the only way we know how at that moment – by crying. We haven't yet acquired the skills of communicating our desires with wisdom but then something from the outside world – our mother - takes us in her arms and gives us what we need, such as warmth, comfort or food. She takes away our feeling of not-okay and we feel okay again, for a while. When we next feel not-okay, we do the same thing and get the same result, i.e. an external something comes along and takes away the not-okay feeling.

So from the moment of birth we have a feeling of not-okay that's taken away by an external source, returning us to feeling okay again. This attitude develops, grows and stays for the rest of our life. When we feel not-okay, we look for something in the external world to come and take it away, such as money, career, partner and material goods. It doesn't occur to us to look within to remove the not-okay feeling, because we have been shown from the moment of our birth that external things take away the not-okay feeling. Is it any wonder that we look externally for our happiness?

Unfortunately though, relying on the external world for our happiness is very dangerous. We become dependent on something that cannot be relied upon. Sooner or later we will react and suffer when the not-okay feeling isn't taken away, or is increased as a result of things that happen. The only way to really retain the okay feeling is to look within and find our happiness and contentment there. We are whole and complete as we are, we don't need anything from the external world to create it. This doesn't mean that we reject the external world. On the contrary, it means that we get *extra* pleasure and joy from it, because we don't rely on it. We enjoy things when they are there and let them go when they no longer work or stop giving us pleasure. We are free from attachment to it and our sense of wellbeing is independent of it as we get our strength from within.

If we are not attached to external sources for our peace, contentment and happiness, we can look at things in the external world with greater wisdom and develop a more unbiased view of them, together with a greater understanding of the consequences of actions. So we might see how eating freshly-prepared food helps our bodies to function better and reduces the likelihood of serious or chronic long-term medical conditions such as diabetes or obesity. We can then *choose* to eat more healthily rather than comfort-eating to make us feel better or live on ready-meals so that we can spend more time working. We can see the value of having a lunch-break to refresh and recharge, rather than having a sandwich at our desk so we can answer more emails.

This doesn't mean we'll never again eat pizza and cream cakes or enjoy a beer. It's not about punishing ourselves or 'doing the right thing'. It's not a duty, or feeling that we *should* eat five portions of fruit and vegetables a day. Instead it means seeing the place for everything and treating them for what they are, perhaps as a treat or pleasure to enjoy occasionally rather than a way of life. It actually *adds* to the pleasure of having them, rather than denying ourselves. Eating healthily then becomes what we *choose* to do, which makes it much easier than the endless round of dieting and then suffering when it doesn't work and we beat ourselves up for being a failure. Again.

Doing something because we *want* to do it and *choose* to do it is much, much easier and more pleasurable than feeling we *have* to do it, or that we *should* do it. Making a choice that comes from within is a much stronger motivation than acting under external influences such as what we 'should' do, or using willpower to force ourselves to do something that we're told is the 'right' thing to do but that deep-down we're resisting for some reason.

Original Fear and Original Desire

Thich Nhat Hanh, the Buddhist monk and Nobel Peace Prize nominee, has an additional perspective on the nature versus nurture debate. When taken alongside the discussion given in The 'Okay' Feeling section above, it can give us a very rounded picture of why we act the way we do. He refers to it as original desire and original fear.

The moment we arrive in the world we are released from the comforting, caring, supporting environment of our mother's womb. Our world is now very, very scary as our needs are no longer taken care of. We are suddenly independent and separate, no longer part of something that feels safe and secure. Even breathing is a new concept that we have to discover for ourselves. This is original fear.

We are born with it and it pervades every moment of our existence unless we find ways to cope with or embrace it. How we act as adults is often a direct consequence of how this all-pervading feeling of fear was dealt with as a child. If we are loved and cared for with wise parents, we learn to use and manage it. But if our parents were unable to do this effectively (although generally not their fault as they don't know any better as it's how they were brought up too), then we live a fearful life. We might not call it 'fear', but when we protect our pride or get angry or depressed we are exhibiting a defense mechanism to the fear. The precise nature of the defenses we employ will depend on our upbringing, experiences, role models, traits, etc., but the root is the same – original fear.

Accompanying this fear is the desire for something to come and take it away. Our original fear reaction is to cry at the top of our lungs but the real desire is actually for something to come and take away the fear – this is original desire. Our original desire will normally be met. We will be fed, comforted, changed or whatever we need. If this first desire is not met we will spend our lives wanting, but our needs will never be truly satisfied because our original desire was not satisfied.

Assuming our original desire is met (and it usually is or we will have died as newborn infants), our first experience of life is that we get our desires met. So we grow up expecting our desires to be met then get frustrated and upset when it doesn't happen. A wise upbringing will educate us that our needs will not always be met, but we will also acquire the skills to know when they might be and when they might not be, so that we can take wise courses of action. This is the root of both the age known as the 'terrible twos' and our sense of adult responsibility.

Being an adult demands that we take responsibility for our actions. In other words, having a mature and wise understanding of our desires and their consequences, so we can take a balanced and responsible approach to life. Achieving this state is actually quite a rare occurrence and if it does happen, it will generally not start to appear until our late middle-ages or when we are labelled 'elderly'. It is the root of wisdom and normally we need several decades of living before we even start to get close to it.

The 'terrible twos' arise because they are likely to be the first instances in life when the infant begins to realize that their needs and desires will not always be met. Lacking wisdom and knowledge, the toddler does not know a way to respond other than by throwing a tantrum. But not only are their needs not met instantly, it also starts to become clear that they are not the centre of the universe after all. They begin to realize that they are in fact separate from everything else. As a newborn they might have looked at their feet and wondered what they were, before realizing that they were attached to them and would do what they wanted them to. But as a toddler they see that people and things are separate and different to them and might **not** do what they want. Now they have to start communicating their needs and desires to something separate from them and hoping that they are met.

Clearly this is a scary and unsettling time for the child. What happens at this stage can be very important in determining how they view the world in the future. A useful technique to help you identify how this stage might have influenced your own development is to try and remember your earliest memories. You won't remember much that happened to you as a two-year old, but even vague recollections can take you closer to what it might have been like back then.

I know someone with an earliest memory of being wrapped in a towel after a bath and then sat in front of the fire whilst their mother lovingly dried them. As an adult, that person views the world around them in a positive light, seeing the best in everything and generally having a very loving and caring attitude.

Two of my earliest memories are of being pushed in a pram by someone other than family members, and leaving home to go to school. I also remember falling into a swimming pool on holiday and being pulled out by someone who was not a member of my family. As an adult I don't feel particularly drawn towards family loyalty and my reaction when things are not going well is to escape – to get away from my surrounding environment, in other words. Given that my earliest memories are of being away from my caregivers and supported by other people, this view is not entirely surprising. I also have anger reactions to situations, which I suspect is from the responses to my tantrums during the terrible twos. As they were responded to with anger (probably – I know what my early role models, i.e. my parents, were like), I learnt that anger was the 'normal' way to respond to things. I didn't know any better and didn't have other role models showing me a different way, so it's not entirely surprising that anger was a predominant reaction in the adult version of me.

Relationships

Our relationships can give us both great joy and immense pain. I'm not only talking here about partners or romantic relationships, there are many other kinds. Some of these are optional, such as our friends, others are given to us, such as family, and a third kind are institutional, such as our nation or employer. It's worth spending a bit of time looking at our relationships with each kind to see whether they give us joy, pain, something in between or a bit of each.

It seems to be part of the human condition to seek relationships, or bonds with other human beings. We have been forming communities ever since we first climbed down from the trees and started living in caves. We feel drawn towards those who appear to be like us ('our' community) but separate from other communities – 'them'. Even within our own community we will feel drawn towards some people and away from others. So relationships are a fundamental part of our being, we have them because we seem to need them and ultimately there is no way to escape from them.

The trick, then, is to look at what we get out of them and what they provide for us. Sometimes, however, it actually helps to view them the other way round. Rather than looking at what we get out of them, we can view them in terms of what we contribute, rather than what they do for us. The three types of relationships mentioned earlier; optional, given and institutional, can be used as a framework for considering our views on relationships.

John F Kennedy famously said *"ask not what your country can do for you, but what you can do for your country"*. The feeling which lies behind this is actually responsible for a lot of the anger and discontent we see around us.

Institutions form because they are mutually beneficial for its members. They are ways of organizing groups of people for a purpose, hence why they're called 'organizations'. But they come and go over time. The current nations in the world are different from those that existed 100 years ago and will be different again in another 100 years. Some countries will split up into smaller groups, others will merge to form larger groups. But it's always about a group of people coming together for mutual benefit. Churches form because a group of believers think in the same way and want to associate with other like-minded people. Trade unions and community groups of all kinds are exactly the same.

But sometimes an organization can institutionally forget its purpose and why it was formed, i.e. for the mutual benefit of the people within. The Catholic Church's abuse scandals are a classic example of this as the clergy focused on protecting the institution of the Church, rather than those for whom the organization was formed, i.e. the people. So the rights of the abused were ignored and the scandals covered up to protect the organization.

Political parties expect their members to follow the party line, i.e. to put the needs of the organization above the needs of the individual members. But political parties are formed to provide strength in numbers for a movement, to make the world a better place (however the party defines 'better'). Making the world a better place means making it better for the *people*, so you can't override the requirements of those same people for the sake of the organization. No organization should be thought of as more important than the needs of the people within it. Its primary purpose is to serve its members' needs, not the other way round.

Not being true to yourself and following someone else's opinion will only ever end in disappointment and difficulty. So before asking what I can do for an institution, I will first of all ask whether the current definition and constitution of the organization meets the needs of the people within it. Then I will consider what, if any, contribution I want to make to it as a body serving the needs of the people. If it meets the needs of members, then count me in. If it doesn't, I'm out.

If we are a member of an organization, we

need to consider whether it considers itself bigger and more important than our needs as an individual. If it does, we run the risk of compromising ourselves and creating difficulties in the future. If we are managing an organization or have a position of influence within it, we need to consider whether we are putting the organization above the needs of its members. If we are, then we run the risk of creating difficulties for other people and sacrificing our own core beliefs which will ultimately lead to inner turmoil and unhappiness.

A classic example of how we might relate to institutions and organizations can be seen in the actions of Jesus. We do not need to be religious or an adherent to the Christian faith to see that Jesus wanted to overturn the rules of his society at the time. He did not feel that they were appropriate so wanted to bring more love and compassion for fellow human beings into the way they operated, hence the overturning of the money changers in the temple and preaching on the Sabbath. However, his solution was not to change the institutions – an external approach – it was to entirely change the way we lived, then more appropriate worldly structures might follow. Unfortunately the vested interests in play at the time would not allow this change, they viewed the preservation of the institutions and 'rules' as more important and crucified him for his beliefs and actions.

We can get great meaning in our life by making

a contribution to institutional relationships that we value and believe are important to our lives. Then it really can be a case of looking at what we can do for them, rather than what they do for us. But for optional and given relationships, we really do need to look at what we give *to* the relationship, rather than necessarily what it does for us.

Often, when we enter into a relationship (particularly a romantic or intimate relationship), we are doing it because it gives us a sense of being complete. We feel whole when we are with our loved one, it's who we've been looking for, The One, our soul mate. But when you start to look at it in terms of being 'complete', you see the logical conclusion of it; we don't believe we are already complete, that we are somehow lacking as a human being and that there is something currently missing from us. If we didn't feel this way, we wouldn't think that the relationship completed us or made us whole. This is actually an incredibly sad indictment of our condition as human beings, that we believe we are incomplete and lacking. If we approach life in such a way – as being incomplete - then we are doomed to a life of unhappiness and dependency, because we will always need to relate to something outside of us to make us whole.

In effect, we are giving our ability to be happy over to an external source. We give the external party our power and say, in effect, "control my happiness –

govern how much of it I can have". This can never be a route to long-term peace and contentment. One day, because the ability to be happy has been given to something outside of us, we'll lose it. Perhaps the other person will no longer act in the ways that make you feel 'complete', or perhaps they'll die. Or perhaps they'll just not be interested in you any longer. And when that happens, your happiness and sense of wholeness will go with it.

If we love ourselves first and realize the wholeness we already have, then we can truly enter into loving relationships. Then neither party will be dependent on each other and instead can give and receive for each other's mutual benefit – we *add* to each other's happiness, rather than detract from it or be the major cause. In this situation we can then look at what we *give* to a relationship, rather than what we get from it. Like self-focus, if we are viewing relationships from the perspective of what we get out of it, we are doomed to unhappiness because one day we won't get back what we deem we deserve, and we'll suffer as a result. But if we give to it, we'll get back in abundance.

This doesn't mean that we act like a doormat though, it needs to act both ways. So if we are truly giving and the other person is deliberately only taking, we have to act with wisdom, which might mean getting out of it. A wise response is needed though. We need to ensure we don't respond with anger or bitterness as that will only inflame the situation and disturb our peace of mind. We can try to understand any delusions the other party may be acting under and then respond accordingly. Understanding, communication and wisdom are the best routes to identifying the most appropriate course of action.

A similar approach can be taken with given relationships, such as with family members or work colleagues. If they are making life difficult for us, we can look first of all at our contribution to see if we are perhaps inflaming the situation. If we are, it will generally be as a result of our own self-focus. However, if they are genuinely causing difficult situations, we need to take a different approach which might involve some or all of the following:

- *Understanding, wisdom and compassionate communication.* If we can see why they are doing what they are doing and appreciate the difficulties they are causing in their own lives by their own unskillful actions, we can think about ways of responding that don't involve anger. It's possible that talking to them about the difficulties they are causing for others may help them to change. Perhaps they genuinely don't realize what they are doing because they are so caught up in their own self-focus. It may be that they actually need help, but don't know how to ask or view it as a sign of weakness.

- *Remove yourself from the situation.* Some people cannot be helped or cannot change their behaviour. Rather than trying and failing, or getting cross at the situation, just don't get involved. You don't have to bail your brother out again, unless you choose to do so. His problem need only be your problem if you decide to make it so.

- *Acceptance.* If the situation cannot be resolved and you cannot remove yourself, then there is no choice but to find coping mechanisms - **for ourselves**. This might be the case where we are trapped in a job or a family member is creating difficulties by their actions. The key point here is accepting that we cannot change or control *their* actions, we can only look at our own response and whether or not it is helpful to our peace of mind and happiness.

Notice that none of these potential routes are about trying to control events or other people's actions. That's because it's generally not possible to do so. The only thing we can really control is our own response. In situations where we might be able to exert some influence, it's about exercising wisdom and compassion, rather than generating more anger and frustration.

Areas for Contemplation

♦ On a scale of 1 to 10, how would you rate your current level of overall wellbeing? What would make it a higher score? What individual events or circumstances would raise or lower your score?

♦ What are your earliest memories? Take each in turn and examine what it says about how you currently view the world. Does it reflect thinking patterns or behaviours in your life?

♦ Are you mainly driven by fear, or desire? If fear, what are you fearful of? Where does this fear come from? What experiences have you had which reinforce this fear? If desire, what are you striving for? Is it an achievable goal that you are actively working towards or a pipe dream? Has it evolved over time?

♦ Identify the different relationships in your life and classify each as given, optional or institutional. Which of them make a real and valuable contribution to your life and which make you feel like you are compromising your core values?

♦ Which relationships make you feel happiest? Which make you unhappy? Why?

Chapter 5

Parables and Teaching Stories

Parables and other stories are an excellent tool to help us understand more about ourselves, the world around us and other people. Often they will be multi-layered to provide multiple lessons but they may also teach alternative lessons to us at different stages in our lives. As we get older a different character may resonate more with us, or the scenario feels more applicable or it explains someone's actions in a way we didn't see before.

In addition to the well-known Parable of The Prodigal Son and the lesser-known Dragon's Tale, there are also scenarios of events which are unlikely to ever happen to you in the format presented, but they get you to think about yourself and how you view the world. Don't rush through this chapter, take some time to reflect as you read and see what they tell you about yourself.

The Parable of The Prodigal Son

You will recognize this story if you had any kind of exposure to religion when you were a child. In the biblical tale, a farmer had two sons. One of the sons – the prodigal one - asked for his share of the inheritance early and decided to go off and pursue his own interests, which generally consisted of wine, women and song. The other son stayed at home to tend the farm with dad. The prodigal son eventually ran out of money and came back home with his tail between his legs. Dad welcomed him back with open arms and threw a big party to celebrate his return. The other son was not happy at this as he considered his brother to have squandered everything given to him. But dad was pleased because now his family was complete again.

Before going any further, stop and have a think about which of the three characters in this story you most closely relate to. Are you like the dad, pining for something lost and will only be happy when the old days come back again? Or are you like the prodigal son who seeks pleasure and frequently needs to be bailed out as a result? Or are you like the stay-at-home son looking after your responsibilities and commitments, but feeling anger and bitterness at the carefree lifestyle of others? Think carefully about this, as it is an excellent technique to help you understand more about the type of person you are. Notice also how these three types are very similar to the three Buddhist personality types presented earlier – Grasping, Aversive and Deluded.

I associated most closely with the stay-at-home son. I am an Aversive type, so related to feeling angry at others for not fulfilling their responsibilities and commitments, as I saw it. The father would be the

Grasping type, holding out for what he believed would make him happy. The prodigal son is the Deluded type as he neglected responsibilities and pursued short-term selfish gains without appreciating the ripple effects on other people.

As an aside, when I first heard this story I completely misunderstood the meaning behind it, possibly because the teachers didn't really understand it either. As well as being a reflection of the three main types of personality, the story in the biblical sense represents what God – the Father – wants, i.e. all his children home, regardless of what they might have done. It is a tale of unity, forgiveness and reconciliation.

Let's fast forward to the present day and modernise the tale. Imagine a mother and father who run a family business and have three children. In this politically-correct era, I'll make them gender-neutral and call the children A, B and C. Being good parents, mum and dad have provided well for their children and give them a financial helping hand at the start of their adult lives.

The first child, A, decides to take the money and spend it, pursuing a life of pleasure and fun. One day, they become part of the boomerang generation and have to come back home because they've run out of money and need the support of the Bank of Mum and Dad.

B sticks the money in a bank account and

becomes very miserly through a fear of losing it. B doesn't go on holidays, doesn't treat themselves to new clothes and generally lives a fairly Spartan lifestyle due to a fear of losing it.

C is very grateful for the money and invests some in new ventures to help the family business expand. C goes on holidays every year, gets a new car regularly and buy presents for people and generally helps out. Not only does C get pleasure from using the money, it is put to good use and accumulates through prudent investments. C's bank balance is much smaller than B's, but C enjoys and gets great pleasure from it, as well as investing something for the future.

This isn't a discussion about money in itself, it's about how you view the world using money as an example. A blows it, like the Deluded personality type with a pleasure-focused, short-term approach to life. B keeps it in the bank and resents the waste they see around them, like the Aversive type. C, on the other hand, has a balanced approach, showing a good mixture of prudence, future thinking, gratitude, sharing – and fun. This book, and the whole concept of 'self-improvement' or personal development, is about making us more like C.

What about mum and dad in this? They might be like either A, B or C. But at this point they have to step out of the equation. They have tried to prepare their children well for adult life but perhaps with mixed success, although this is unlikely to be solely due to them. At some point, the parents have to release control and let the children make their own way in the world, allowing them to make their own mistakes. They can guide and support, but ultimately it's up to A, B and C to make their own choices and follow their own path. Perhaps though, they can be like the father of the prodigal son, celebrating their successes but still providing support when needed. But the one thing they can't do is live their children's lives for them.

The poet Khalil Gibran in *The Prophet* sums up the role of the parents nicely in this. He likens the role of parents to an archer. They can prepare the bow and arrow perfectly, ensuring their aim is true, but at some point they need to release the arrow and let it fly. At that point, it's out of their control what happens although they might need to make themselves available to pick up the pieces if things go awry.

A Dragon's Tale

I first read this story in the writings of Jack Kornfield of the Insight Meditation Society and it had a lasting effect on me.

In an ancient kingdom a long time ago, it came time for a beautiful young princess to marry. Unfortunately, her father the King had to have her betrothed to the local dragon as payment for some long-forgotten curse. The Princess did not know what to do but one of her ladies-in-waiting told her to visit the old lady of the village who would give her appropriate advice. This she did, and duly prepared for her first night as a married woman.

The wedding day came and gave way to the wedding night. The Princess said that she would gladly give the dragon her love but he had to do something in return. He agreed as it was either that or live out the rest of his days as a lonely old dragon with no-one to talk to or keep him company. She asked the dragon to remove a layer of his scales and in return she would remove a layer of her clothing.

Layer upon layer were removed by both parties, causing immense pain and discomfort for the dragon, but he knew he had to proceed – his future wellbeing depended on it. He desperately hoped the pain and discomfort, the anguish and torture of removing layers of scales, then hard flesh, then skin becoming successively more raw and tender would be worth it.

Eventually he removed all his layers to reveal what was underneath – a handsome, charming prince who was cursed long ago for the wrongdoings of his own father, sealed in a dragon's body until a fair maiden offered herself willingly to him.

Rather than just being a very politically-incorrect but traditional fairytale, there is layer upon layer of meaning in this story.

First of all, we have the duties of family loyalty, potentially making us do things we would rather not do or don't know of any alternative, just like The

Great Swindle. So we start off being fairly clueless about life, taking whatever comes our way because we don't know any better. We may also be cursed by the 'sins' of our parents and families, i.e. whatever they do will have an impact on us and the rest of our lives. We are cursed or blessed or something in between by them and their actions.

As a result, we put on layers of armour – the dragon's scales. This armour appears to keep us safe but in reality it prevents the real person from being revealed and achieving our full potential. The process of removing these layers makes us feel vulnerable and painful but we feel drawn towards continuing the process. This is explored in more detail later in Chapter 7 - The Process of Healing.

Like the princess, we are driven into our lives not really knowing what to do or where to turn for advice. But the ancient wisdoms – the old lady in the village – are there to help us. But we have to follow the advice rather than thinking we know better. Had the princess not followed the advice, she would not have worn so many layers on her wedding night and not asked the dragon to start shedding his skin, so that the real prince could be revealed. Then the ending may have been very different.

More than just a fairytale, this story presents a complete picture of the path to finding peace.

The Hostage Situation

Imagine that you are caught up in a bank robbery with a number of other people and you are all taken hostage. The kidnappers decide to show the police they mean business so ask for a volunteer to be killed. The hostages include you, a mother and her young child, a doctor, a banker with plenty of money, a farm labourer, a homeless junkie and a suspected local paedophile. The kidnappers offer a choice; either someone steps forward willingly, or the group has to select someone.

Stop and think at this point; your immediate reaction is very important. Do you step forward to be killed and save the others, or do you think the group should decide? If the group decides, who do you think it should be?

Many people state at this point that they would offer themselves. This feels very admirable and is what many of us think we 'should' do, but it conceals two very real issues. First of all, in that situation when your life is at stake, what would you *really* do? Even though there's a rich banker, a junkie and a paedophile in the group? If the answer is still a definitive "yes" then well done, Gandhi and Jesus would be proud of you and you are worthy to be in their company. But most of us would actually be paralysed with fear and confusion, before our self-preservation instinct kicked in.

If you're not as altruistic as Gandhi but still feel that you should offer yourself then you might want to examine issues around self-esteem and guilt. We often think that we 'should' feel that way but the truth is that deep down we have decided our life is not actually worth as much as other people's. We might not voice it or like to admit it, but deep down it is how we truly feel.

If we didn't offer ourselves then we might want to look at how judgmental and opinionated we are. Did you pick the junkie? What if he was due to start rehab today and is in the bank to withdraw his benefits before travelling to the residential clinic – does that change your mind? Or did you pick the paedophile? What if he's actually on trial but hasn't yet been convicted although local outrage has convinced everyone he's guilty. What if he's actually a paediatrician and the local community got the name wrong and mistook a child doctor for a child molester - would that change your opinion?

What about the doctor – he must be a good person, surely? But what if he's Doctor Shipman, Britain's biggest mass murderer or a drunk who is about to be exposed for his high death rates on the surgeon's table?

Did you choose the banker or farm labourer? As you don't know anything about their lives, why would you pick them? Perhaps the banker runs a fair-trade organization providing micro-credit to small rural businesses in Africa, helping them to get out of poverty without aid handouts. Maybe the farm labourer is actually the son of a wealthy Russian mafia boss who is on a gap year and is doing the labouring as a rejection of his father's values.

But surely there couldn't be anything wrong with the mother and child? Again, you don't know them. Perhaps the child has been kidnapped by the woman and is on her way for the child to be trafficked into slavery. So maybe the mother should be picked for execution.

Haven't a clue what you would do in this situation? That's a good answer and reflects the majority of the population. They really do not know what they would do, but are still happy to give an opinion anyway.

The Drug Thief

In this scenario, a pharmacy has been broken into and drugs stolen. Your task is to decide on the degree of punishment for the offender. Read through the statements below and identify whether the additional knowledge presented in each would change your opinion, and at which stage. Try to identify the stage at which you think the offender should not be prosecuted or the severity of the punishment should be reduced.

1. Crooks, thieves and robbers should always be punished to uphold the values in society and standards of common decency.

2. The thief was a 14 year old boy, caught red-handed with the drugs in his pocket.

3. The stolen drugs were prescription painkillers and other medical treatments, rather than substitutes for illegal drugs such as the heroin substitute methadone which could be sold on.

4. The other drugs taken in addition to the painkillers were drugs used for the treatment of cancer.

5. The boy's mother is currently undergoing treatment for cancer.

6. The boy's mother has recently had her benefits stopped so that her address cannot be traced as the boy's violent and abusive father has recently been released from prison.

7. It is the boy's first ever brush with the law and he and his mother escaped from the violent father 13 years ago.

8. The boy was so nervous as he committed his first crime to get his dying mother's pain-relieving cancer drugs (and only the amount needed for his mother's treatment for that week, no more) that he left his fingerprints and other forensic evidence everywhere.

Most people will have decided by the end of these scenarios that sending this boy to jail is probably not a good idea. Most of us have enough compassion to actually want to donate the money his mother needs to get the life-saving drugs, rather than putting her son through the criminal justice system in such tragic circumstances. The real question is when you made the switch. Being closer to levels 1 to 3 might highlight one of two things; either you are very compassionate, open and understanding, or you have an unrealistic view of society and are regularly taken advantage of. The closer to stages 7 and 8 you were before you made the switch, the more likely it is that you are quick to judgement and may not investigate situations fully and thoroughly before forming opinions.

Only you will know the level where your view began to soften, but the exercise of assessing where you made the switch can help with identifying your view of the world and how you relate to it.

Areas for Contemplation

♦ Which of the parables and teaching stories do you most relate to? Why?

♦ Taking each story in turn, which character do you most strongly associate with? Why? Is your answer likely to have changed over time?

♦ Can you see the characters in other people you know? What is the effect on them and you of acting in this way?

Chapter 6

A Map of Our World

The Road Less Travelled by M. Scott Peck was mentioned earlier in the context of emotions but it also has another useful concept on how we view the world, which pulls together many of the concepts discussed so far. During childhood we learn the ways of the world and our place in it. In effect, we are creating a map of the world. But it's not actually ***the*** world, it's ***our own*** world. Every individual will have their own map, different from everyone else's. When maps are similar, we have agreement and harmony. Where they aren't, we have conflict.

This map is how we view the world, our guide to the rules we follow and how the world operates. By the time we reach late teenage years or our early 20s, it is usually fairly fixed. Unfortunately though, the world is continually changing which means that our map will already be out of date by the time we have it. Or perhaps it was just plain wrong in the first place. Either way, if we are using an out-of-date, inaccurate map, it's very hard to find our way around. We will get lost or take very ineffective routes.

As we get older and lose the flush of youth, the effects of this out-of-date, inaccurate map will be experienced more and more. Perhaps we have a mid-life crisis where we realize that we haven't achieved what we'd hoped or it feels like all our dreams have failed to materialise or things 'go wrong'.

We will find the reasons for this in our map. If we are aware of what our map is telling us, we can see which areas are inaccurate or unhelpful. This is what the book has been about so far, i.e. trying to identify what our maps look like and why, together with how helpful they are for the future. With these answers we can look at what will give our life meaning in the future. As with using any map, there will be indicators available to illustrate where we are, which we can then use to get our bearings and know where to go next. We can use many of the concepts already presented so far as indicators, but there are others such as our personal role models, health, sleeping patterns and use of external stimulants.

Personal Role Models

It would be a real gift to see yourself as others see you – and there are ways of finding out. We can look at our previous role models to see the type of person we have become, plus the current people we admire (who are, in effect, our current role models), and the company we choose to keep.

Past Role Models. If you want to know more about who you are, look at who brought you up.

Whether we like it or not, we reflect our parents and guardians. As very young children we don't know how to behave or respond to the world, so we model what we see around us – and that's our mum and dad (or whomever brought us up, such as extended family or institutional carers). If they are loving and supportive, we tend to view the world in a benevolent, caring way. If they were anxious, we worry. If anger and aggression were dominant themes, we'll have them.

It is sometimes the case that we become the exact opposite. If we were abused, for example, we may go onto become very loving and have a career in the caring professions. Or if our parents were alcohol-dependent we may become teetotal. If our parents had wealth we may become charitable but if they were poor we become ambitious and focused on money. But generally, we mirror many of the attitudes we experienced as children from our closest care-givers.

So if you want to know how other people see you, look at who brought you up and it might start to give you a very good indication.

Current Role Models. Who do you admire? Is it top business people with their wealth and power, or is it nurses and carers? Do you look at the winners of sporting events or the coach that runs the local kids team? Observe the characteristics of the people you look up to. You are likely to already feel the same way (ambitious, competitive, etc.) or are striving to be more like them (caring or community-minded perhaps). These feelings will be reflected in your daily speech and actions.

The company you **choose** *to keep*. You can't pick your family and may not be able to pick your work colleagues either, but you can choose your friends and with whom you spend time with outside of work and family obligations. You will feel drawn towards some people and environments because they reflect something in you. So if you find yourself surrounded by aggressive, competitive people then it is possible that you are similar. If you are drawn towards loving, caring environments, you are either likely to be this way yourself or are striving to be.

These aspects; our role models (both past and present) and the company we choose, can tell us many things about ourselves, but we have to be honest and true about it. It's not about finding out what's 'right' and then trying to do more of it. Instead it should be an open analysis done with loving-kindness towards yourself - you may be very uncomfortable with what you discover. It is a tool for self-knowledge, not something else to beat yourself up over.

Health and Sleeping Patterns

Our general health, sleep patterns and use of external stimulants are great indicators for our map of the world, how we are doing and where our issues may lie. Some health issues naturally befall us, such as those that come from accidents, but many of them are created by ourselves and how we view the world. Aches and pains such as backache generally come from how we live. For example, I have back trouble because I have been so stiff and rigid throughout my life. I am stiff, literally, both physically and in the way I think. I have skin problems because of how I relate to the world – it is my outer connection with the world and as I have problems with how I relate to the external world, it manifests in ugly blotches and reactions, much like how I view the world.

Digestive problems come from the food we eat and how we treat our bodies. They are a consequence of what we do. If we do not engage with our emotions and bury them, we are not in tune with our gut feelings. So the gut reacts in an unhelpful way. If we push our bodies to do more than they are capable of doing they will rebel and make us do what's needed, so we get stress reactions and illnesses, or we get colds and infections that make us stop and slow down. But how do we react? Do we take some drugs and carry on? It's as if we are trying to dictate how our bodies should react. Unfortunately the body won't listen and it will eventually win. It will *make* us respond to what it needs. Recurring or regular health issues should be treated as a wake-up call, not an inconvenience. Those which cannot be diagnosed easily by medical professionals or that do not respond well to standard treatments are also signs that something is out of balance.

I used to think that I was grumpy and bad-tempered because I was stiff and sore. But I realize now that it's actually the other way round. If I'm feeling sore and stiff, then it's because something is nagging and irritating me, there is something in my life that I'm not happy about. So I investigate and usually the pain eases when I find out what it is and deal with it. If this investigation doesn't reveal anything then I accept that it's something medical so visit the doctor for medication.

There is a technique from therapy and meditation called the 'body scan' which involves going through each part of your body to try and identify where there might be tension, pain, or some other physical sensation. If you are in tune with your emotions and physical sensations this can be a very useful technique in identifying areas of your life where there may be unresolved issues or that are causing you difficulties. Discomfort in the lower back, for example, may indicate something related to how secure we feel, whereas a slight headache might indicate rising stress levels or worry. Noticing your heartbeat can indicate rising anxiety, then we can investigate what we are feeling anxious about.

Our natural sleeping patterns should fit into one of two categories. We either sleep solidly and peacefully for between 6 and 8 hours at one stretch, or we need two shorter periods per day of continuous rest. When we lived in caves it seems we might have got up at dawn and been active during daylight, then slept for a period. We would then wake later and engage in social activities such as discussions around the campfire before sleeping again for another few hours. We were more active in summer months when there was more light but slowed down and became sluggish in the winter when there was less light, warmth and food with our bodies responding as if they were in semi-hibernation. If we're not naturally following one of these two patterns (either one long sleep at night or two shorter ones throughout the day), then there is something wrong with the way we live. We are not treating our body effectively and it will react accordingly. Ironically, not sleeping is a wake-up call, like recurring health issues.

There are two main sleep problems from which many of us suffer; either we can't get to sleep, or we wake in the middle of the night. Many of us deal with these by using some form of external assistance. We might have a drink at night because it helps us to relax and fall asleep, but the sugar in the alcohol will give us an energy spike between 2 and 4 in the morning meaning we wake up, unable to get back to sleep with our mind working overtime. And then, because we're tired because we haven't slept well, we take stimulants during the day to keep us going, such

as coffee, chocolate or other refined sugar products.
This creates another energy spike which we then need
to come down from so we have a drink to relax. We
have created a cycle of 'uppers and downers' that is
very unbalanced and dangerous for our health.

The only way to break the pattern is first to see
it, then take action. If we are in this pattern of uppers
and downers it is a sure sign that our life is unbalanced
and that there are issues somewhere that need
resolving. The core of the problem isn't that we use
uppers and downers, they are just the symptoms and
are natural consequences of how we live. The issue is
why we need them, as it's a sign of something needing
review.

Areas for Contemplation

By way of summary, let's recap some of the
components which will constitute our view of the
world, our map. You might want to think about which
are most significant for you and whether they are
positive things that you want to make more of, or
areas where your current approach is perhaps not as
helpful as it could be.

> *Role Models* – how have these influenced you in the
> past and which do you feel most drawn towards
> now? What does this tell you about yourself and
> are you happy with it?

Emotions – are you in touch with these or have you been suppressing them? Which ones are particularly strong for you?

Thinking Patterns – do you exhibit any negative or unhelpful ways of thinking?

Personal responsibility – are you able to take personal responsibility for your actions and reactions? Do you feel life is under your control or are you dominated by events?

Delusions – which are your strongest?

Self-focus – are you self-obsessed or aware of other's feelings and emotions around you? Do you care about other people or are they tools to help you get what you want?

Upbringing – how did your childhood and subsequent events influence your view of the world?

Personality – are you an aversive type or more of a grasper or deluded? Which of the personality schemas do you feel most closely describes you?

Internal or external focus – are you neurotic or character-disordered?

Having answers to these questions will help give your life meaning, which is the topic of the next section.

Part Two

Changing Our World

The previous section explored why the world is the way it is and why we are the way we are. By itself, this knowledge can be very useful and helpful. It's as if awareness of a situation and the reasons behind it are enough in themselves to give us relief and a way forward. I've heard this described as 'shining the light of awareness'. In the same way that shining a torch illuminates a space so that it is no longer dark, knowing why we are the way we are can be enough in itself to provide great meaning and hope.

But the real benefits come when we take this knowledge and actively think about how to use it for our benefit. This section takes the areas covered in the previous chapters and highlights how they can be used to help our lives. This is where the individual pieces of the jigsaw begin to fit together. How your own jigsaw will look is something you need to establish for yourself, but hopefully this part will give you guidance on how you might do it. Don't take any of it as a 'solution' though, look instead at whether it is likely to have value for you in your situation, then adapt and use it as required to suit yourself.

If you have studied science, you will know that making a change to a formula produces a different outcome. Altering the process, timings, ingredients and sequence can all create completely different compounds. Even small changes can make big differences. Changing our lives is the same. If we always do what we've always done, we'll always get what we've always got. So if you want something different, you have to change the formula. This is also the root of the psychological concept of stimulus-response. This means, in effect, that everything has a consequence so the secret is to identify the stimuli and resultant response, then we can break the reaction so that we get a different result.

But to do this we need to stop and think. Thich Nhat Hanh describes this process as stopping-calming-resting-healing and it's a bit like the phrase; 'when you're in a hole, stop digging'. We need to find the time to stop, even for a moment, and consider what's happening. Looking calmly at a situation will help us to see why we have arrived where we are and what we might do next. But we can't do that when we're busy and frenzied. We need to stop, calm down and take some time to rest and recover first. A useful technique for doing this is mindfulness, or awareness of what we are thinking and how we are feeling at any point in time. This is covered in more detail in the Meditation, Mindfulness and Awareness section of Chapter 11.

Chapter 7

The Process of 'Healing'

This concept can be a bit misleading at first glance. It implies that there is a formal set of stages to go through – a process – in order to achieve a feeling of being 'healed'. There isn't a 'process' and there is no mythical state of being 'healed', but it can help to identify what you might experience as you move through the journey, so that you know you are not alone or unique in feeling these things.

What's the Problem? Many of us go through life with expectations which are sometimes met, but often aren't. We usually have a general feeling of dissatisfaction and unhappiness but we don't realize it as such, we just think it's normal. It's why many of us do the lottery, because we feel that if we won the jackpot all our problems would be fixed and everything difficult would go away. You will see this type of reaction around you frequently. It helps explain why the world is the way it is, i.e. that we haven't really got a clue and we just carry on doing what society tells us, separating and judging and suffering as a result. At this stage we are like lemmings or sheep, we just keep carrying on with what we're 'supposed' to do or 'should' do. As Dory, the absent-minded fish in *Finding*

Nemo sings, "just keep swimming, just keep swimming".

Is this it? At this stage we become aware of the general feeling of dissatisfaction and start looking for something else. We begin to realize that we have been like sheep and followed the 'rules', but it hasn't actually made us very happy. We might have the career, house, car, partner and some money in the bank, but we're still looking for something else. We need a bigger house, better car, more money, a younger and prettier or more caring partner, more responsible job. We know something is missing, we know we need and want something else, we just don't know what it is. An analogy for being at this stage is like having a stone in your shoe. Something doesn't feel right and it's a bit uncomfortable but you can't see it. But you know that you will have to stop and do something about it at some point, otherwise you'll just get more and more irritated.

We might become aware of entering this stage when we reach middle-age or a significant birthday and start reflecting on what we've achieved – or 'failed' to achieve. Alternatively we might have a serious accident or illness that makes us re-evaluate ourselves and our lives. Many significant life events can also trigger this feeling, such as redundancy, children leaving home, illness of a loved one, death of a parent, etc.

What am I Looking For? Having realized that

something might be missing, or having a vague feeling of dissatisfaction, we start exploring. We might seek a new career or have a midlife crisis. Or we might start reading self-help books or dabbling with religions or new hobbies. This is the stage when men might want a Harley Davidson motorcycle, for example, others might seek cosmetic surgery or want a new look or makeover. What we feel as 'loss' is actually the natural ageing process and we miss the flush of our youth, so we seek ways to get it back.

Digging up the Pond. If your life journey takes you down a self-exploration route, you will reflect back over your life and see the things you've done and the things that have been done to you – the memories. I call this 'digging up the pond' because you may be exposing some fairly horrible stuff that has lain untouched for a long time. But the problem is that it hasn't been dormant, it has been giving off noxious, toxic fumes. What you thought was a hard life and a general feeling of dissatisfaction with the world is actually your own poisonous fumes hanging around you. And the only way to clean it up is to dig into yourself.

This is where 'healing' really lies, for it is only by digging up the pond that you get rid of all the muck, clean it out and have beautiful fresh, clear water in its place. The Christian mystic, St John of the Cross, calls this the 'dark night of the soul'. Many people stop at this point because it is just too painful and difficult. The trouble is, once you start you won't feel 'healed' until it's done. If you start you have to finish, otherwise you'll have the existing noxious fumes **and** a half-finished process to contend with. Not only will the pond still stink, you'll now notice how much it smells, whereas you didn't before.

Anger and Upset. If you've ever looked at the stages of bereavement you will be familiar with the different thoughts and feelings that people go through after losing a loved one. When we embark on the self-exploration path, we go through a similar stage in that we 'lose' our old identity, our old way of viewing the world, and it can make us angry. For me, it involved getting angry at The Great Swindle. I felt I had been duped into what I was supposed to do in life and I had a sense of waste at having lived life inappropriately for so long. Others might be upset at losing the old map of the world they had. At least they knew where they stood and what they were doing – but not now.

Acceptance. If we are on a motorway journey and find we are going in the wrong direction or miss our exit, we might get angry and upset, just as in the previous stage. But when we accept that we've made a mistake and then head in the right direction, we can relax again and start to enjoy the journey. We might even see other opportunities that we want to explore, but either way we know we are headed in the right direction now, and it feels good, after the anger or upset subsides. We can relax into it and enjoy it.

But there is the danger of becoming stuck at this stage. We love the new-found knowledge we have and are very proud of what we've discovered and what we've changed about ourselves. But we then start to form a revised identity around the new version of ourselves which creates a different set of problems. The analogy is the addict who describes themselves as 'a recovering alcoholic' 10 years after they last had a drink. They're actually an *ex*-alcoholic, they've already recovered and there is probably less chance of them relapsing than there is of anyone becoming an alcoholic. But they're stuck in the past and not moving forward to develop themselves further and reach their true potential. This isn't acceptance, it's stuck in fear. A ship is safe in the harbour, but that's not what it was made for.

Healing. There are at least two schools of thought on this. The first is that we suddenly 'get it'. Everything becomes clear and we know how the world works and why we are the way we are and what to do with the rest of our lives. Japanese Zen Buddhism has a word for this – '*satori*', which is like a flash of enlightenment.

Most of us are not fortunate enough to experience a *satori* and we have the second approach to healing. We just make our way through life, generally feeling better about things and getting wiser, without realizing that we are. It's only when we reflect on how we used to be, or find ourselves in a crisis and being the calm one, knowing what to do and helping everyone else out without getting stressed ourselves, perhaps where we give strength to others rather than needing support, that we realize just how far we've come. We may also look around and see how far we might still go, but that's okay, because things feel good and we're enjoying life again, rather than battling it.

Even without a *satori*, we sometimes get flashes of insight when we realize something significant. Things click into place and we might realize why something happened the way it did, or why we feel the way we do, or what we need to do next. It has a 'resonance' as it feels right, as if it's in the correct place. As we explore ourselves and start to see the world around us differently, we will get these more and more often and they keep us going. They are like checkpoints or milestones on a journey that indicate we are still going in the right direction and that we are continuing to make progress.

These flashes of insights can come to us in a variety of ways. They might be in dreams, or a thought that suddenly pops into our head, or even in songs we hear or movies we watch or chance encounters. It might be a line in a book or magazine that we read. When they happen we often dismiss them and say; 'I wonder why that happened?' or we might call it a coincidence. But what's actually happening is your deepest-self telling you something.

Our night-time dreams are reflections of what we're thinking about. Sometimes it's just routine processing of what happened during the day but we probably won't remember much of this as it will feel like a jumbled mass of unintelligible 'stuff'. But sometimes a dream will stand out and we will remember it when we wake. It's worth noticing these as it will be a message from our emotions. Write down what happened as soon as you can and then take some time to explore what it might mean. There are plenty of dream interpretation websites that can give you hints and tips of what certain symbols and images in dreams mean, but don't take these as facts or true. Instead, use them as inspiration for what it might mean for you as an individual. The only person who can interpret your dreams is you, but other people can give pointers on what they *might* mean.

I tend to get random songs playing in my head. I used to dismiss them as just tunes (I like listening to music and do it a lot) but sometimes one will play over and over again, especially one part or a few lines. When this happens I stop and think about what it might mean. I remember a comic song that used to frequently pop into my head. I had only heard it a couple of times at a music festival so I wasn't remembering something recently heard on the radio.

The song was to the tune of *Walking in the Air* but the singer changed the words to "I'm turning into dad". Then I realized that I frequently acted in the same way as my father would. I was, literally, turning into a version of my dad. I used this knowledge to keep those aspects of his behaviour and attitudes that I thought were helpful and useful, but discarded those parts that weren't.

Another example is someone I know who gets random movie clips. In one instance, she was trying to meditate but kept being interrupted by a scene from *Titanic*. Try as she might, the image would not go away. In the end she gave up on the meditation session as her mind kept drifting back to movies. It was only later she realized that the movie clip was in fact describing her relationship with certain family members. The clip was memorable for her because it reflected how she felt. So when she took the time to sit and reflect, the image came up as a visual demonstration of how she actually felt.

Gaining these insights can be likened to unpeeling layers of an onion. Each time we realize something, we acquire a greater understanding of ourselves. Removing a layer also reveals what lies beneath but which was previously hidden, like the dragon's scales from the story in Chapter 5. So we keep digging and investigating, acquiring more understanding as we go, identifying things that we didn't even realize were an issue until we started on the journey. Sometimes the insights will come fast and furious making us think that 'enlightenment' is just around the corner, but we will also go through periods where nothing much seems to happen.

We will also encounter periods when we reach what I call an 'edge'. This is when we come across an insight or the reason for feeling a certain way but something about it doesn't quite sit right. It's a bit too uncomfortable. My edges often come about when I am looking at how to alter my thinking patterns or my overall view of the world. I came across an edge when I realized that my upbringing led me to always want to control external situations. I'm very achievement-oriented so am always looking for the action that needs to be taken to resolve a situation or the fix for it. So asking me to accept that life was outside of my control was like asking me to cut my arm off. It pierced through to the very core of who I thought I was and my strongly-held view of how the world operates.

My solution to the edge was shining the light of awareness on it, i.e. realizing that this was how I truly felt. I had built my entire approach to life believing that I if tried hard enough and wanted something badly enough, I would get it, that a 'successful' life was within my grasp and under my control. Telling me anything else was a very difficult message so I rejected it. But over time I began to realize that I wasn't losing or sacrificing control as I never actually had it in the first place anyway. You can't lose something you never had. Realizing this edge and the lunacy of what I had been trying to do all my life was very painful at first as it turned everything I believed upside-down, but getting over this edge was actually very liberating and was a key component of my personal jigsaw. The lead up to this edge and the immediate aftermath were both fast and furious periods of insights, although I got stuck in the middle moving from one view to an alternative.

I've found in my journey of personal exploration that I keep going back further and further in time. I started with exploring the present to see how I currently felt but then realized that the way I felt at this moment was a consequence of the previous moment, so back I went, right to the time when I was in my mother's arms. I realized that I had picked up energy patterns from her which are still present in me, such as a frenetic and active mind. Ultimately what I realized was that everything I currently am came from something in the past. There was no core 'me' or personality that I was about to uncover, I'd acquired all of it. I actually found this incredibly liberating as it meant there were no rules, and instead I could create myself the way I wanted to be for the rest of my life.

But that gave me a problem, because I had no idea who or what I did actually want to be. I knew what I wasn't, but not what I wanted to be or could be. All I had to go on were the rules I had been given

– the Great Swindle. I knew they were inappropriate and unhelpful, but I didn't really know what ***would*** be more helpful and useful. And that's where I currently am - reinventing myself, but I don't really know what to yet. It's actually really quite exciting and feels very creative and liberating.

How Long Does it Take?

It takes as long as it takes. It might take a whole lifetime, or perhaps you'll have a sudden flash of insight that brings clarity, light and understanding to your life. I can't put a time on how long it has taken me to reach my current stage because it's hard to pinpoint when it actually started. But if we take my interest in Buddhism and therapy as the starting point, it took about 10 years to fully realize who I was and that I could be who I wanted to be. I don't know how much longer it will take before I've 'reinvented' myself, mainly because I don't yet know what that will ultimately look like.

The process of discovery and creation becomes easier when you stop forcing it and let it happen. It's as if the act of looking for it prevents us from seeing or 'getting' it. There an old Buddhist saying that when you have one eye on the goal you have only one eye on the path, which means you're more likely to trip up. For those of us with an achievement-orientation or control tendencies this is really hard, as we want to make it happen. We think that having decided what needs to be done and the 'right' way, it should happen instantaneously. We don't want to wait so try to rush it and get disheartened when it doesn't happen quickly enough. It's the psychological or spiritual equivalent of saying 'are we nearly there yet?'.

One of the curses of our age is the 'microwave mentality'. Like a ready meal that can be heated up in a few minutes, we want everything now because society tells us we can have it. We can't. Good things take time and effort.

It's much better to relax and enjoy the journey. Then we might realize that there *is no journey*, that we have already arrived and have everything inside of us that we need, right here, right now. Chasing after something newer, better, different means we miss what's there in front of us, what we already have – and have always had, if only we'd known.

I've found the book *The Mindful Path to Self-Compassion* by Dr Christopher Germer a great help in explaining the process of healing. It also starts to illustrate how long it can take. Dr Germer outlines the stages of healing (or self-compassion as he calls it) as aversion, curiosity, tolerance, allowing and friendship. These labels are not quite self-explanatory so the meaning of the stages is given below.

Aversion – this is similar to denial or resistance. At this stage the event or need for healing has started but we refuse to accept that there is anything 'wrong'. We can't possibly be doing anything wrong, it's everybody else's fault. If only *they* would change, everything would be fine. At this stage we might be reading about self-help or spirituality and think it's all nonsense or not helpful, but something might be nagging us, making us carry on with it. It's like the stone in the shoe analogy mentioned earlier.

Curiosity – at this point we move out of Aversion and begin to wonder if perhaps it might have something to do with us after all, or think we might be able to do something different. We begin to think that maybe, just maybe, not everything is someone else's fault and that perhaps we might possibly have something to do with at least some of it. This is the real start of our journey.

Tolerance – now we're beginning to accept that many of our problems and circumstances are in fact down to us after all. We've brought much of it on ourselves, or the situation cannot be changed so we need to find ways to live with it and find coping mechanisms. We've started to dig the pond and accept that it's not a pleasant job, but we'll find ways of dealing with it.

Allowing – at this stage we accept that we have a whole variety of emotions and feelings around something but rather than fighting them or looking for

141

coping mechanisms, we observe them. As we see them coming and going and begin to realize more about them, we develop understanding. At this stage we're truly accepting, rather than seeking coping mechanisms.

Friendship – this is where we realize that there is nothing 'wrong', that everything is just a sequence of cause and effect, of consequences, and we move through life with this knowledge. We realize that other people aren't a problem, that our emotions aren't in themselves the issue, that everything is fundamentally okay if we just let it be and not try to control it. There's nothing to 'cope' with as it's all part of the rich tapestry of life and we can use our experiences to bring both understanding and comfort to others who might be suffering. Now we're embracing the way the world is and are in touch with our common humanity, rather than trying to find ways of dealing with our 'problems'. We let life find its natural flow and embrace the results, rather than trying to make things happen in a certain way or make our happiness conditional on a specific set of external conditions.

In the book, he outlines the case of a woman who lost her child to illness. She went through all the stages and Dr Germer met her around 20 years after the event. By that time she had come to accept the loss of her child and now used the feelings to help other mothers who were in the same situation. She never got over the loss as such, nor would it ever be expected that she did, but in the act of realizing that she could use her experience to help others in a similar situation, it gave her incredible comfort in realizing that she wasn't alone and could actually use the loss of her child to help others. But it took nearly 20 years to reach this point.

Areas for Contemplation

♦ Which stage of the healing and exploratory journey would you say that you are at?

♦ What are your barriers for moving to the next stage?

♦ Do you have any recurring images, songs or dreams? Spend some time investigating what you think they might mean.

♦ The next time something pops into your head 'out of the blue', think through what it might be telling you about yourself and your life.

♦ The next time you remember a dream, write down the details as soon as you can. Spend some quiet contemplation time thinking through what it might mean. Is it reflecting something currently happening in your life or is it giving you direction on a path you should take?

◆ Where do you encounter your 'edges'? Why is it an edge - what's difficult to accept or change about it? What benefits might you encounter if you were to view it in a different way?

◆ Can you identify what first triggered the feeling of 'there must be something more?' What was going on in your life at the time?

Chapter 8

Changing Thinking Patterns

A recurring theme in this book is that many of our problems arise from the way we think. It follows, therefore, that we need to change the way we think if we are to make our lives happier and more peaceful.

The first stage and most fundamental building block in changing our thinking patterns, is to be aware of what we're thinking and the consequences of it. The practises of mindfulness and meditation explored later in this book will help with this, as will the 'Areas for Contemplation' at the end of each chapter. Without awareness of what we're thinking and the consequences of it, we cannot change anything and will continue to do what we've always done, meaning that we'll always get what we've always got. In other words, no change.

Five useful concepts in helping to change the way we think are 'trauma bolts', 'RAIN', 'PRADA', hot thoughts, and healing words.

Trauma bolts

Pema Chodron, a Canadian single mother who became a Tibetan Buddhist nun, writes about the concept of a 'shenpa'. She describes a shenpa as a way of thinking that hooks us in and is difficult to get out of, like a fish that gets caught on a baited hook.

Shenpas are the situations in which we always react the same way. They are the types of things that make us say 'I couldn't help it', or 'why do I always mess up?'. It could be, for example, that we get angry when our mother expects us to visit, or to drop everything for her latest crisis even when where we are busy. As soon as it happens we feel our hackles rising, our blood boiling and we know that anger and frustration are the inevitable results. When the 'crisis' is over, we are still seething. Mum might be happy, but we are cross. Or perhaps our boss calls us in and we immediately begin to feel scared. We worry that we have done something wrong and that we are about to get into trouble or even lose our job.

We can also think of our shenpas as our buttons. Press one and a reaction will be triggered. They create an emotional feeling within us, but one which is repeated whenever a similar situation arises. I have coined the term 'trauma bolt' for the cause of these shenpas. I call it this because they arise from something that happened in the past that emotionally affected us (a trauma), and a bolt because it seems to come out of nowhere very quickly and hits us with enormous force, like a bolt of lightning.

Using mindfulness and awareness of our emotions, when we feel a shenpa arising we can investigate the source of the trauma that created it. In my own case, I was bullied at school. There were occasions when I was beaten and punched simply by being in the wrong place at the wrong time. In one instance, I was walking across a thoroughfare where older boys (about 16 years old) used to play football. I was about 12 at the time but there was no other way to get where my friends and I wanted to go. One boy kicked the ball at goal just as I was passing and it hit me, so he punched me in the face three times for stopping him from scoring. As well as the pain and blood, I clearly remember the feelings of helplessness and vulnerability, the unfairness of it all. I wanted to get back at him, to lash out, but as a 12-year old with no older protector, I couldn't. I had to live with it. This event, along with similar occurrences, has seethed within me for decades – but often silently. I don't regularly remember the event, but I realize now that I do get the *feelings* associated with it.

Now, in my early-50s, if someone verbally lashes out through anger or makes me feel helpless, it recreates that same pain and vulnerability inside. I want to lash out too, through anger and upset. It is the equivalent of the psychological concept of Post-Traumatic Stress Disorder (PTSD), although the term is usually used in relation to soldiers returning from conflict or following a major accident such as a car crash. In time, the fall-out from an event can become a trauma bolt and create a shenpa. It creates a way of responding – fear and anger - that seems to repeat itself and becomes a part of us.

One technique for dealing with it comes from a Buddhist technique explained by Thich Nhat Hanh. He calls it "hello Mara". Mara can be thought of like a shenpa, but in physical form or as a personal demon. So when we feel a shenpa arising from a trauma bolt, it is Mara – one of our demons - coming to visit and torment us. But rather than getting fearful or angry at the visit, we can say; "hello Mara, come and sit with me for a while and talk, so I can learn more of your ways". In this way, we realize that a shenpa has been activated but rather than lash out in our usual way, we investigate it to find out where the trauma came from.

I know where my shenpa of frustration, upset and helplessness at other people's anger comes from now, I can see the memories. But I can also see it for what it truly is – memories that trigger a habitual response. Having discovered the cause, the trigger for it, I can learn to respond in a different way. By shining the light of awareness on the feeling and reaction, I have brought it into the light where I can learn more about it and consider different ways of responding. I can also see the same reaction in others and develop compassion towards them as a result, rather than my usual anger response.

This technique won't work immediately, but as we learn more about ourselves the instances of trauma bolts arising will decrease and, when they do arise, they will be less intense and pass more quickly.

RAIN

This follows on from the concept of investigating what caused the shenpa to arise. RAIN stands for Recognition, Acceptance, Investigation and Non-Identification. I first came across the concept from Jack Kornfield of the Insight Meditation Society.

Recognition. This means recognizing that a shenpa or trauma bolt has arisen and that we are responding in our usual, but unhelpful, way. Mindfulness is needed to recognize how we feel and what's happening.

Acceptance. This is accepting that the situation or shenpa has arisen, but it doesn't necessarily mean that we accept what's happened or been done to us. It is not a passive state of resignation. We are not doormats. It's not acceptance of someone trying to get us to do something against our will or that we don't feel is right or appropriate. Instead, it's acceptance that we *feel* a particular way. The opposite of Acceptance in this instance is Denial, rather than Resistance. So it might be that someone gets angry at us and we lash out in return. We accept that we are angry at the situation, rather than pretending that we're okay and that it didn't affect us. Or, if it is someone trying to get us to do something against our will, we realize and accept that it makes us feel uncomfortable, rather than blindly going with it.

Investigation. Because we've realized that a feeling has been triggered within us, we then probe and poke around a bit to find out why we feel the way we do. This could be where we discover the cause of our trauma bolts, the deep-seated emotional memories of an event that are triggered by the current circumstances. Therapy can help with this, as can meditation or reading about psychological concepts.

Non-identification. In this stage we realize that we are not the feeling, instead we are a person who **had** the feeling following an event, as a result of a set of circumstances. So rather than habitually getting angry or anxious, we have broken the cycle of always acting in a certain way. We might still **choose** to act in the same way, but now it's a conscious, deliberate choice, rather than an instinctive reaction.

These four stages work together sequentially. Before we can identify what's at the root of a feeling or emotion, we have to recognize that we have the feeling and stop denying it. Then, when we know what's caused it, we can see whether the reaction is helpful for us and in what circumstances, giving us wisdom about ourselves and how to act in different situations.

It also works well with the technique of "hello Mara". When we recognize a shenpa arising, we can identify where it's coming from and investigate it further. But like the previous technique, it's not one that will necessarily give immediate relief. We can start the process immediately, but the act of investigating may take a long time and involve a lot of painful memories.

PRADA

This has nothing to do with handbags or shoes. In this instance, PRADA stands for Pause, Relax, Attend, Deal and Arrows. Unlike the other two techniques, it *can* be used immediately for instant benefit, but it still needs mindfulness and awareness.

Pause. When something happens that triggers a reaction or sensation, whether a deep-seated trauma bolt or an everyday occurrence, the first thing to do is stop. Rather than acting blindly or habitually, we pause before doing anything else. A second or two may be sufficient, or you might need to remove yourself from the situation for a bit longer. However long it is, it should be just enough to stop the habitual reaction before you do it. Mindfulness is essential for this, so that we feel the potential reaction but have sufficient awareness not to act on it immediately.

Relax. Good decisions and responses are not made under feelings of anger or frustration. It's better to calm down first, and relax. This might mean taking a couple of deep breaths or counting to ten, or it could be removing yourself from the situation for a few minutes or a couple of days, until you calm down, relax and are able to deal with it more calmly.

Attend. Now you are more calm and in a better position to think clearly rather than through your traditional habitual way of reacting, you can review the situation and decide what to do. The first step is to investigate what caused the problem. This could involve finding the reasons why it made you feel the way it did, or why the situation arose. Either way, it's something that you can learn from. Then you can decide whether taking action is appropriate and the most effective form of response. It might involve you doing something, or replying to the person that caused the reaction, or it might be choosing not to take action and instead investigate what caused you to react in the way you did. You would move into the Acceptance and Investigation stages of RAIN.

Deal. Having thought through what to do about the situation in the Attend stage, now you're ready to act. But there are actually only two emotionally-healthy responses you can have to anything; either take action or accept it.

Taking action is only viable if whatever you plan on doing is helpful, either to make you feel better or to change the situation. Be careful of acting on delusions at this point though, such as looking for revenge. It needs wisdom to identify what is truly helpful. Your habitual reactions may not be helpful, otherwise you might not have felt the need to read this book. Be careful of trying to control people or situations here, this step is about what *you* need to do to improve *your* situation, not change someone else or act in a self-focused way to the detriment of others.

If there are no actions that can be taken, or if they wouldn't create any real benefit, then you have to accept what's happened and get on with your life. To put it bluntly, if it can be fixed, then fix it. If it can't, find ways to get on with your life and take joy in what you have, rather than bemoan what you've lost or don't have. But don't wait for something to happen to bring you happiness, be happy and grateful now for what you do still have. This is the real meaning of the Biblical phrase, "seek and ye shall find". Seek happiness and contentment within yourself rather than from outside sources and you'll find it.

Arrows. This relates to the Buddhist concept referred to earlier of the two arrows; one is the event itself and the other is that which we plunge in ourselves afterwards. Be aware of any arrows you are putting into yourself and whether you are twisting the blade, i.e. your reaction to the situation.

Hot Thoughts

This is a technique from Cognitive Behavioural Therapy which helps us identify what's really at the root of the way we feel. As with many techniques, it needs mindfulness as its starting point. When a feeling arises, such as anger or anxiety, we need to first of all recognize that it has arisen and then investigate why we feel that way about the situation. It is likely that there will be a number of contributory factors and lots of things going on in our head so the first step is to record these, perhaps by writing them down. Then we can investigate what we are truly fearful of, perhaps by asking 'why am I afraid of that? What's the consequence I'm scared of?'. The anxiety might be fear of messing up at work, then losing our job which will lead to losing our home. At some point we will get to the real root of it, which might actually be a fear of being made homeless, forgotten about and unloved. This is the 'hot thought', the one that really creates the feeling.

We can then give a rating to the feelings, perhaps as a percentage such as 80%. We should also try to identify all of the feelings and thoughts around the issue and give each a rating. This rating serves two purposes. First of all, when we think about the hot thought and consider it more logically and rationally, perhaps by identifying potential solutions or realizing that it is irrational, we might find that the anxiety feeling naturally subsides. We can then give a revised rating to the new feeling and might want to record the outcome in a journal. Over time, we will see repeating patterns of thought but also how the feelings are subsiding, which gives us a powerful motivational boost.

The second purpose is that by rating different feelings we can identify which are the most significant and important, so work on them first. This is equivalent to breaking problems down into manageable chunks that we can more easily deal with, rather than being overwhelmed by everything. How do you eat an elephant? One bite at a time. This is the same principle.

Healing words

Affirmations are sometimes given in self-help literature as a tool to help us improve by developing positive thinking. Often they will be something such as; "*I am calm and strong*" or "*money comes to me easily*". I think we need to be really careful with them. The danger is that they might remind you of what you're not, so all you actually see is your own perceived weaknesses being reinforced. If you tell yourself that you are calm and strong but in reality you end up a blabbering wreck at the slightest thing, you'll just make yourself feel worse. If your debts increase even though you try really hard then you will experience a feeling of failure, rather than money coming to you easily.

So tread carefully with them. It's much better to use statements of fact to remind you of the way things actually are, or to provide aspiration for what you're trying to achieve or be. Perhaps instead we could create statements or mottos, rather than trying to affirm anything. As you progress along the journey you will find those which feel most meaningful for you. My favourite approaches are given below.

'This too will pass'. This reminds me that everything is temporary. If I feel good at this moment, the thing I feel good about will end at some point so I can exercise gratitude for it and enjoy it more, but by the same token if I feel bad that will also change. I use variations on this theme depending on the circumstances, such as 'the sun always rises in the morning, even if you can't see it'. Even after the longest, darkest, stormiest night, the weather will stabilise and it will eventually get light. Always. It's just a case of waiting, although you may need to deal with consequences afterwards as it might have created a 'new normal'.

All activities and feelings occur in cycles and it's relatively easy to see it around you, if you take a longer term view. Sports teams, for example, go through periods when they are at their peak then they start to decline. In time they will rebuild and may go on to greater things, then they will start to decline again. In a work setting colleagues and managers will come and go, sometimes creating a harmonious, balanced environment and sometimes conflict, but then in time it will change as the managers and colleagues move on and other people join the team.

'May I live with a sense of comfort and ease, free from a frenetic mind'. This statement comes from a Buddhist concept called metta, which means loving-kindness. In this case, it's about loving-kindness for myself. Rather than an affirmation telling me what I'm not, it reminds me of what I'm trying to achieve and what I'm working towards.

Notice the language used in it. First of all, the phrase *'May I'*. It's not saying that I am, or that I will be, as these things are outside my control. Instead it states how I would **like** to feel. Secondly, *'a sense of'*. It doesn't say which things I need to have which might give me this feeling, such as money and good health, as these may also be outside of my control or have other consequences. Instead it is asking for the *feeling*, and that **is** within my control. There are no conditions on it so the achievement of it is completely in my hands. It reminds me of what's important and how I'm trying to train my mind.

'Things can always be worse'. No matter how depressed I feel or how bad things seem to be, the universe has a knack of showing me someone who has it worse. I might be feeling down after a day at work or having had an argument with someone and I'll turn on the news and see a devastating earthquake or typhoon that's killed hundreds and left many thousands homeless without food, water and shelter. Or I'll watch a movie with child cruelty, or rape used as a

weapon of war or people being bombed and tortured and suddenly my situation doesn't seem so terrible after all. I can then feel quite grateful that I have a job and that all I've got worked up about was someone cutting in front of me at a roundabout on my drive home. If you want a sense of perspective on your problems, visit a cancer ward or sick children's hospital and maybe your situation won't seem so bad.

'There's always a choice'. This can be hard to accept if you're trapped in a horrific situation or the consequences of an option seem unpalatable. But you can usually step away. You might not like what it will lead to, but you can still do it. When the consequences of stepping away feel worse than staying, it's amazing how it frees up your mind to develop acceptance rather than bitterness and helps your mind to look for ways to improve the situation, rather than escaping from it.

'It's only your problem if you make it your problem'. This applies when dealing with other people who are continually asking for your help or if you have a strong need to control. If someone is asking for my help and I'm glad to give it then it's not a problem. But if I think they are taking advantage or putting their stress and irresponsible behaviour on me, I don't have to accept it. It's their behaviour, their stress, their needs - not mine. Unless, of course, I choose to help, then I'll gladly do it as it's my choice, rather than feeling I have

to. I'm amazed at how many things I'm happy to do now after applying this way of thinking, where previously I would have got annoyed at the inconvenience.

'*You might die tomorrow*'. This sounds depressing but it is very true. You might not even stay alive long enough to finish reading this book. Most readers will still be alive tomorrow, but some won't be – and you might be one of them. So if you were going to die tomorrow, what would you do differently today? What's stopping you? What a wonderful way to live more in the moment and get a true perspective on what's really important and valuable to you.

Be a bit careful with how you respond to this though. It is likely that you will still be alive tomorrow and possibly for many more years to come so you can't abandon everything. You will still have commitments and responsibilities, there will still be dependents to look after, food to put on the table and bills to pay. But if it helps you to establish your priorities you might be able to do with them a fairer grace and more joy.

'*Don't judge someone until you've walked a mile in their shoes*'. It's very easy to compare ourselves to others and generate jealousy or low personal self-esteem, or alternatively to condemn and judge. But we really don't know what someone else's life is like, or what's going on in their head, or how their upbringing has affected them, or whether their family life is harmonious. So perhaps we should lay our judgements aside and instead seek understanding so that we can develop compassion and wisdom.

'*Starfish on the beach*'. I use this remind to me of a story I read in *Chicken Soup for the Soul* and the lesson behind it. A man is walking along a beach in Mexico one day after a heavy tidal surge which has washed thousands of starfish onto the beach. As far as the eye can see, there are stranded starfish, unable to get back to the safety of the sea. Amongst this sad sight he sees a young boy picking up starfish one by one and putting them back in the water. He goes over to him and says "why are you doing that? You'll never make a difference with this amount." So the boy picks one up and places it in the sea. "It made a difference to that one", he says, before picking up another and putting it too back in the safety of the sea, where it belongs.

As well as teaching us that children have an innate wisdom that we forget about as 'educated' adults, it also illustrates how we can get overwhelmed by what we see around us. We can't make a difference to the whole world, but we can make a difference to ourselves and those we come into contact with. In fact, that's *all* we can do, make a difference to ourselves and our world, moment-by-moment, day-by-day, every day.

'A ship is safe in the harbour, but that's not what it was made for'. My life experiences, starting in childhood, have made me risk-averse and fearful. I suffer from anxiety and worry. If I stick to my faithful routines and try to control everything, or so my reasoning goes, then everything will be fine and I'll be safe. But I'll also miss out on many joys in life and new experiences. By staying safe and not trying anything new, my life may not be as rich and joyful as it could be. If the ship puts to sea it may well encounter rough water and other trouble, but that is what it was made for. By the same token, by trying to stay safe I miss out on what life has to offer me and I fail to see the new experiences which could greatly enrich my whole being and help me achieve my full potential.

'What is this telling me?' This is useful when faced with the minor inconveniences that we are all presented with. It might be a cold that prevents us from doing our usual activities for a few days, or we can't make something happen at work or with family members and get frustrated at it. Our usual response is often to try and make the problem go away, but perhaps we need to look a little deeper at what's causing it. Perhaps we have caught a cold because we are feeling run down or trying to do too much, so it's actually telling us that we need to rest for a while and slow down. Or perhaps we're not acting skillfully with our colleagues and family members so are not able to

work in the best ways with them.

Areas for Contemplation

♦ The next time something 'pushes your buttons', use the techniques of PRADA and RAIN to help identify why it created a reaction within you.

♦ Are there any 'trauma bolts' that you know of? Why do they affect you in the way they do?

♦ If you have recurring feelings of anxiety, fear or depression, use the hot thoughts technique to help you get to the root of what's causing the feeling. Use PRADA and RAIN to help.

♦ Which of the healing words and phrases had the biggest impact on you? Why?

♦ Which of the phrases would it help you to remember most in your daily life? You might want to pin them on your mirror or write them on a card to keep in your wallet or purse as a reminder. You could even take a relevant photograph or cut out an image from a magazine if it helps you to remember it.

Chapter 9

A New View of the World

As well as changing our thinking patterns, we can also develop different attitudes, giving a newer, fresher, more helpful way of viewing the world. As with changing our thinking, if we change our attitudes to something more virtuous, our personal world will naturally change with it.

Forgiveness

We sometimes think of forgiveness as being an external thing we give to other people – "I forgive you". But the dictionary definition of forgiveness is actually very different. It means 'to stop feeling anger or resentment', so actually has nothing to do with how we view other people, but concerns the feelings we hold within ourselves. To forgive means we stop feeling anger or bitterness about what has happened to us, and instead accept it, and move on.

To *not* forgive something means we hold all that anger and bitterness inside ourselves. Whether we forgive or not often makes absolutely no difference to the person or event that we deem responsible for our suffering and pain. It still happened, they still did what they did, and we still had to cope with the consequences. None of that changes, but we *feel* better as a result. Holding on to resentment and anger merely creates bitterness and stress and can lead to illness if held for too long.

I suffered with back problems for a long time as a direct result of holding myself too tight, too rigidly. When I loosened up and accepted what had happened to me, my back had a chance to recover its natural flexibility again. But this could not happen whilst I was holding on to anger from the past. I had to forgive to recover, but not other people, *me*. I had to accept what had happened to me, see the consequences of it, realize that it wasn't helpful and then move on.

Nobody knows that I have 'forgiven' them, nor do they care. It is a personal thing for my own healing. I once heard a story about an ex-prisoner of war who was asked if he had forgiven his captors. "No, never !!" was his reply. Then they still hold you captive, he was told. He is still bound in his mind by what happened in the past, still held prisoner. Not by the captors, but by his mind and attitude towards his past.

Some of the greatest political and societal leaders of the 20th century have needed forgiveness to achieve what they did. Nelson Mandela, for example, had to leave bitterness in his prison cell before he could become the President of South Africa and the Truth and Reconciliation Committee could never have done its work to bring the country together. Ang Sun

Suu Kyi needed to forgive being separated from her family and held under house arrest before she was able to bring Burma back into the worldwide community. Both Gandhi and Martin Luther King had plenty of things to forgive after the hatred, imprisonments and beatings inflicted on both of them. But they did, and left the world and their countries as better places. So forgiveness isn't a weak-willed, wishy-washy thing, it is an incredibly powerful and strong action that can create massive improvements in people's lives, both your own and others through the ripple effects it creates.

By the time we reach middle-age we will have encountered many problems in life, many difficulties. This is an important cross-roads for us. We might become bitter and angry so move into older-age feeling upset and frustrated at the world, probably leading to illness and being a cantankerous, unpleasant old person. Alternatively, we could use the experiences to generate wisdom within us so that we become more pleasant, wise and a joy to be with. We can assist other people with our wisdom and compassion, rather than getting angry and frustrated at everything.

Forgiveness and acceptance at this stage are vital to our future well-being. Together they allow us to move more into wisdom than anger. But it's related to us, not to other people. Forgiveness is not an external step, it is an *internal* feeling and action.

There are two other aspects necessary for forgiveness; seeing the situation in terms of other people's delusions, and our own self-focus.

There is an illustration from Buddhism that demonstrates seeing the situation in terms of other people's delusions. If someone hits us with a stick, we might get angry with the person but the stick is actually as much at fault as the person. We view the stick as having no control as it is wielded by someone else who has power over it, but the person is as equally out of control as the stick is. When we are controlled by our delusions we act mindlessly and do not see the consequences of our actions. In effect, if we are under the influence of delusions we have no control over what we do, so the person wielding the stick does not know what they are doing. They can't help themselves, in the same way that we can't either when we are under the influence of strong delusions. So we could exercise compassion and understanding of the person, rather than resorting to anger. When we can see the situation from their perspective we can see why they did what they did, and in doing so realize that getting angry and holding bitterness is not helpful.

The second aspect, self-focus, follows from this. We might be hurt physically by the stick, but mentally our suffering is caused by how we view the situation. Our pride and indignation can prevent us from seeing what's really going on and the reasons for it, so we develop anger, bitterness and feelings of a need for revenge. But all this does is destroy our peace of mind and fuels our own anger. You cannot be angry and peaceful at the same time. We could try instead to seek a wise, understanding response that helps the situation, rather than acting under our own self-focus and delusions to perpetuate the situation. This is how feuds and vendettas arise, by allowing ourselves to be governed by self-focus and delusions, thus developing anger following unskillful and unhelpful actions by others.

When we find ourselves drawn into a cycle of anger, bitterness and revenge, the solution is forgiveness. This is what happened with the Truth and Reconciliation Committee in South Africa after the end of apartheid. Rather than seeking revenge fueled by anger and hatred, the parties came together to disclose and discuss what happened and then sought appropriate solutions that allowed people to live together peacefully in the future. The root of this was forgiveness – releasing the anger and bitterness for what happened. But remember that forgiveness does not mean accepting what the other person did, it may be that the wise response does involves some form of punitive measure or redress for what has happened. Societies will still have methods for punishing those who break that society's rules.

Lessons From Addiction Programs

I've thankfully never had to take part in any

addiction programs but I have read about them and have seen lots of aspects of them that can help people generally. The most useful points I've personally found helpful from them are shown below.

Submit to a Higher Power. This can appear confusing and misleading at first glance because of the connotations with God, but this isn't what it means. Instead it's about accepting that we can't control the world around us. Addicts often suffer from worry and anxiety as a result of trying to control external events and people. When this inevitably fails it leads the addict to 'escape' through the object of addiction. In effect, they give their personal power and core inner strength over to a drug or some other source. The 'higher power' refers to something 'higher' in worth and value than the object of their addiction, rather than meaning higher than them as an individual. The ultimate high power is the universe itself, which cannot be controlled, but it can be enjoyed and appreciated. If we accept what the world throws at us, life can be much easier than trying to resist it and failing.

One day at a time. This could equally well be termed 'one *moment* at a time'. So rather than worrying about the future or dwelling on the past, concentrate on this moment, only this moment, and open to what it has to offer. We cannot control what will happen next, but we can use mindfulness to see what is happening in *this* moment and appreciate it for what it is.

Focus on Other People. This is the same as releasing self-focus. If we concentrate on others and show compassion for them, we're not so caught up in ourselves and our own dramas all the time. It's not all about us.

This is a big aspect of many addiction problems. The individual is very caught up in their own world, seeing only the impacts on them and taking everything personally, from a very external perspective. The perceived threats from the outside world make them retreat further into themselves and they think only of themselves rather than taking a wider view. Anyone who has lived with an addict will recognize the self-focused approach they have. Concentrating on other people helps to reduce this emphasis so that they think less about themselves and see some of the impacts of their actions on others. By not being so caught up in themselves and their own needs, it reduces the desire to escape inwards via the addiction object.

Kindness and Compassion

Love and compassion are the exact opposites of self-focus as they involve a focus on others. But they don't mean sacrificing your own needs for the sake of everyone else's and being a doormat, they are actually about developing understanding, tolerance and a caring nature towards others.

Everyone experiences good and bad times in their life. If they're good now, bad things will happen in the future and if times are unpleasant, things will pick up eventually. It might take a long time and involve a lot of suffering, but even after the longest, darkest, stormiest night, the sun will still rise the next morning.

This is exactly what's happening to everyone else around you. They are going through good and bad times, suffering and pleasure. Some of it will seem self-inflicted and at other times it will appear to be very bad luck.

If you think you're having a hard time, look around you and put yourself in the shoes of the starving, the destitute, the homeless as a result of disasters, the bereaved, prisoners of conscience, the kidnapped, victims of crime and accidents who are now disabled, the parents of severely disabled children. See their suffering and pain, and feel it for yourself. Still think you're having a hard time of it?

Now think about the burglar, the junkie, the alcoholic, the violent criminal, the welfare cheat. Are they happy people? Imagine the torture and pain going through someone's head before they break into a house. Think how desperate, worthless and valueless as human beings they must feel, to be able to inflict that on someone else. These are not happy people.

Yes, they make you suffer by their actions, but they're doing it because they're suffering themselves.

Their minds are tortured and full of self-focus, paranoia, anger, hatred, bitterness, jealousy. Not a happy place to be, not a happy world to live in. They're doing these horrific actions because they are driven to it by their tortured minds, destroying their peace and happiness, thinking that it's the right thing to do when all it's going to do is cause more suffering. Not only for you, but for them when they go to prison, lose everything around them, have their self-dignity removed, suffer violence themselves from people in the company they keep and then live in poverty when they're found out or kicked out the home. Every addict, prisoner and homeless person will have a harrowing tale of suffering to tell.

So what causes all this suffering? Self-focus, anger, intolerance, pride, jealousy – and sometimes bad luck. You too may have self-focus, anger, intolerance, pride and jealousy. Those you may condemn have exactly the same feelings and thought patterns as you, although perhaps in a more extreme way. They have also been presented with a situation where the thoughts and feelings can be (or *need* to be, in their self-focused opinion), acted out. Maybe you have simply been fortunate enough not to be presented with the same set of circumstances or bad luck.

This is where love and compassion for everyone (not just the 'deserving') comes in. We all live by delusions and suffer as a result. The saying "there but for the grace of god" is absolutely true. There indeed, go you. Perhaps not now, but you will in time. Try looking at those around you who are suffering or inflicting suffering on others and see if you can see aspects of yourself in their actions. See when your thoughts are similar to theirs, such as jealousy, perhaps, which is what burglar might be feeling when they want what you have. Remember actions of yours from the past that have caused other people upset. Listen to your words and hear if they spread love, joy and happiness, or anger, gossip and bitterness. Think of your motivations and see if they are self-focused or of an understanding, caring nature.

Look at your judgements and those you may condemn and think deeply about why you hold that opinion of them. Does it actually reflect a fear you have that you may end up the same way, or a tendency that you yourself have? We often find that the things which annoy us in other people reflect the things we dislike about ourselves. So if we dislike people with a controlling attitude, for example, it may be that our own nature is to try and control people and situations. That which annoys and upsets us is often a mirror for ourselves, or a deepest fear speaking out.

Is it any surprise that the world is so full of pain and suffering when our thoughts, words and actions make it so? And yet we blame other people for our problems rather than looking at ourselves to see what delusions we live with and create. We get upset when people inflict actions or words upon us as a result of their delusions, but we don't see the exact same delusions in ourselves. The degree and scale might be different, but not the root. Anger and jealousy are still anger and jealousy.

It's very easy to feel love and compassion for people when you can see something of yourself in them. And when you feel love and compassion, you'll see better and understand more because you're not looking through the eyes of anger, paranoia and self-focus. That understanding will bring the wisdom that leads to peace and happiness because you will know what to do in any situation to make things better for everyone concerned, rather than worse. Anger, intolerance, hatred, bitterness and jealousy will only ever create more problems.

Kindness helps you to reduce the biggest delusion of all - self-focus. It's not possible to be self-focused when you're doing something for someone else. The second major benefit of kindness is that it fills your mind with good stuff and increases your overall positive nature, leading to positive benefits in the future. Thirdly, spreading a little happiness makes the world a generally nicer place. Finally, looking for acts of kindness helps you be more observant of the world around you and increases your overall wisdom and awareness.

It doesn't have to be major acts of voluntary

service, little acts are sufficient. If you open your eyes and your mind to it, you will see people in a queue who are fumbling to find change, or struggling to get upstairs with shopping, or waiting to get out into the flow of traffic, or looking for directions, or a million other little things. Make someone's day by helping them out and bring a smile to their face.

I once saw a sign outside a church which said; "what have you done today to make God smile?" That's probably one of the best ways to describe it. If not for their sake or God's, do it for yours.

Follow Your Dream

Find a passion that stirs the soul and follow it, rather than concentrating on the job, career, house, etc. Ignore what society tells you about what gives you happiness. Find what really stirs your soul. It might be music, art, sport, science, caring, engineering - or even careers such as business or law. Then revel in *doing* it. But don't do it to *achieve* something, such as money or to be the 'best', simply try to enjoy the process of doing whatever 'it' is. This leads to loving every moment as time is spent doing the things that stir our passion, that feed our soul. What an incredibly satisfying way to live.

The inevitable difficulty with this approach is, of course, that we still need to earn a living. We still need money to buy the things for our passion (materials, for example, if it's art), plus a place to live and food to eat. But the difference is that we would then be seeking jobs and occupations that provided *this income*, rather than careers and jobs taking over our lives and distancing us from our family and common humanity. It is also distinctly possible that we might even be able to make a good living doing our passion.

For many of us, particularly if we are a victim of The Great Swindle, we won't know what this passion is. We will have been channeled down a route of career and progression, met a partner, bought a house and had kids, then find ourselves in a mid-life crisis, wondering how we got where we are. We look at the hopes and dreams we had when we were younger lying in tatters all around us. Perhaps we were good at art as a child, or enjoyed music or writing but were encouraged instead to pursue our exams and a career – "get a proper job". I like the concept of 'dream-stealers' to represent this concept, where well-meaning parents and teachers guided us to what they thought we should be doing, rather than allowing us to find and follow our passion.

But the dream-stealers don't have to win or dictate your life. This doesn't mean we abandon our responsibilities, we are adults and have to take personal responsibility for our actions and circumstances. It doesn't mean abandoning our mortgage payments and children to go off and become a surf-bum. But it might mean restarting things we enjoyed when we were younger. Perhaps we might

175

have enjoyed colouring as a child, for example, which we might now turn into painting or making jewelry or model-making. Perhaps our love of music leads to us taking up a musical instrument (which we do for pleasure rather than achievement) or we join clubs and societies.

If you are a parent or teacher, you might want to investigate how far you steal dreams. Are we guiding our children down the route of achievement with *our* view of success and 'what's right', or are we allowing them the freedom to explore and experiment, to take time to find out what really fires them up and stirs their soul? If we want to give them the opportunity for real happiness we could let them play and discover themselves, then facilitate opportunities for them to do it.

As an adult, we will probably have to spend some time thinking about what our passions might be or even experimenting with different things to see where our interests lie. This is something that a life-coach can help with, especially if we want to set up a plan for making it happen.

Having a passion may also lead to greater joy and energy-levels in older-age. We sometimes see older people parachute-jumping or running marathons and hope that we are as fit as them when we reach that age. When asked what the secret is to living to an old age healthily they might answer that it's having a little glass of whisky or a drop of olive oil or some other 'miracle ingredient'. But perhaps it's nothing more extraordinary than living their passion and this allows them to carry on into a ripe old age. They have a reason and a purpose to life and that's what drives and inspires them. Not having a passion and viewing life as a struggle is guaranteed to drain you over the decades, removing your ability to live a fit and healthy old age.

I heard a story once of an important visitor being given a tour of a new hospital under construction. The visitor asked one of the workers what he was doing. "Laying bricks" was the reply. The same question of the next worker was answered; "making a living so that my family have a home to live in and food to eat. I'm hoping for some overtime so I can also take them on holiday". The third worker replied; "I'm contributing to my local community by helping to build a place of healing where sick people can come and be looked after and their families can come and visit them in their time of need". Same job but three attitudes – which approach do you think is most likely to create a happy joyful life? Which do you have?

We can think of our energy and zest for life as being like a bucket. Our bucket may be full when we are young but as time goes by we dip into the bucket to keep us going, so we use up our supplies. As well as emptying the bucket, there may also be holes through which our energy leaks over time. These holes are the attitudes which do not serve us well, such as anger, hatred and bitterness. By the time we reach middle-age our buckets are often empty, leaving us feeling tired and exhausted with life. If we change our attitudes we can repair the holes in the bucket but we also need a way of replenishing our supplies. Following our dream and living a life full of purpose and meaning is how we refill our buckets.

I saw a very moving news article regarding the death of the oldest known survivor of the Nazi holocaust death camps. The lady died at 110 years of age having gone through horrors most of us daren't even think about. But there were two things that stood out for me when they broadcast an interview with her. The first was the statement that 'life is beautiful'. This from someone who had experienced the horrors of Auschwitz. Secondly, she said that music was her life. Even though she was in her nineties when the interview was recorded, she still played piano beautifully. What greater proof can there be that having a joyful attitude and finding a sense of meaning is the secret to a long and happy life? She found something that ensured her bucket was well and truly filled, having been completely drained at an earlier stage in her life.

Many people go on to develop new careers and do their greatest work from their fifties and sixties onwards. Many of the great spiritual leaders and visionaries didn't start their true calling until well into their later years and then carried on for decades afterwards. Nelson Mandela was 72 when he was released from prison. The Dalai Lama is over 80 at the time of writing. Thich Nhat Hanh and Pema Chodron, both of whom have been discussed in this book, are in their 90s and 80s respectively. Their buckets seem to be well and truly full and going strong. The reason is their attitude and having a purpose in life.

For many people, following your passion will sound very woolly and impractical. The pressure of having to make a living and meet family responsibilities may well mean that returning to your passions is simply not possible at this stage in your life. I found this particularly difficult to deal with when I discovered I had been caught by The Great Swindle and, like an insect in a spider's web, I felt trapped.

The route to a feeling of freedom involved looking carefully at my life and what I had, then evaluating what I thought of it. I asked myself what I would have chosen if I could do things differently and start again. I took myself away on retreat so that I wasn't caught up in day-to-day distractions when I did this. I then realized that if I could do it all again, I would probably have chosen most of what I currently had. The family, job, house and the other big life things were all what I would probably have chosen if I were to do it again. Obviously there are issues and problems and some things that weren't ideal, let alone 'perfect'. A bit more cash would be nice, working a few less hours would be good too, an extra holiday occasionally would go down well, I wished I was a bit fitter and I'd like some people around me to stop complaining quite so much, but overall it was broadly fine.

If you do the same exercise you might come to a different conclusion. In this case I would suggest returning to some of the other exercises in this book and review whether you are going to choose acceptance of what you have, or whether there are actions you can take to improve your situation. But be very, very, careful here. Are you acting out of self-focus, or wisdom? If you're acting from a position of deluded self-focus you are likely to leave a trail of destruction in your wake and in a few years' time you will find yourself back with the same feelings as you have now, but with a different set of circumstances. You need to find a core inner strength as that's where true happiness lies, rather than in your external circumstances.

It seems we need a threshold level of circumstances before we can find peace. Until we have this minimum level of satisfaction with our outer circumstances, it's very difficult to feel calm, happy and at peace with the world. If we are living from hand to mouth and genuinely wondering where the money to pay this month's rent or heating bill will come from, we are unlikely to be thinking about much else other than that. We certainly won't be considering anything as woolly as living your dream or following your passion, other than in daydreaming moments. But there isn't an absolute minimum of acceptable circumstances, it's individual to each of us. A millionaire can have the same level of fear and anxiety about losing everything as a single mother living on benefits.

There is a principle from psychology that demonstrates this called Maslow's Hierarchy of Needs. This is often represented as a pyramid with our basic survival needs at the bottom (food, water, shelter) rising up through needs for sex and loving, communities and relationships through to self-actualization at the top where we achieve our highest potential. Maslow does not acknowledge where the minimum level is to achieve 'happiness', only that we continue to strive upwards but can only do so once lower level needs are met.

The problem is that we set the bar of the minimum threshold level too high. The lower the bar of expectation, the easier it is to meet, thus freeing yourself up to follow your dream. But the higher we set the level needed, the harder it is to achieve and the greater the likelihood of living an unsatisfied life. Trying to achieve the unachievable as a condition of your happiness is complete madness. Ironically though, it seems that when we do achieve inner peace and strength, the threshold level becomes irrelevant as we are happy and contented regardless of our external circumstances. We are then free to follow our desires but without conditions attached to our happiness.

Finding your passions and filling your soul with them is one of the ways of feeding and developing your core inner strength. Even if you can't make a living doing them, you can still seek opportunities to do as much of it as you can. If you identify the aspects of your job that you enjoy you might be able to find a way of doing more of it. For example, if you enjoy meeting new people perhaps you could ask to meet more clients or see customers more regularly. Or, for those parts that you don't like, find ways to reduce the time spent on them or to make them less onerous. You might look at time-management techniques to find ways to complete those jobs you dislike sooner, so that you have more time to spend on the things you do like. If you get strength from nature, go to work via the park in the morning and feed the ducks or watch the squirrels. If you like sport, take your kids to a local game on a weekly basis or take them to a club and join in yourself.

Remember also that happiness and peace are feelings, not objects. If we don't *feel* happy then by definition we're not happy. If you do more of the things that make you happy and fewer things that don't make you happy then there is only one possible result; more happiness.

If you use mindfulness and meditation to identify your likes, dislikes and threshold requirements, you will build up a picture of what truly stirs your soul. Then put your mind to finding ways of doing more of the stuff you like and less of the things you don't. For those things you don't like, either change them or practise acceptance as they are ultimately part of a bigger picture of how your life looks, they are a natural consequence of where and what you are.

Coping With Major Life Events

It is inevitable that we will have to cope with major trauma in our life. Unless we die young, the majority of us will have experienced most or all of the following by middle-age:

- Death of three immediate family members (two parents plus a sibling or child)

- At least one significant partnership breakdown

- A period of relative poverty with all its implications – property downsizing, impact on standard of living, etc.

- Redundancy or other job loss or difficulty

- Serious illness or accident to ourselves

- Serious illness or accident to loved ones

- Physical symptoms of growing older, i.e. failing

eyesight, hearing loss, tooth decay, greying hair, stiffness of joints.

In addition, depending on our circumstances, we might also have the following:

- Children not following our wishes or otherwise disappointing us

- Death of other close relatives such as aunts, uncles, cousins, grandparents and close friends

- Burglary or violent crime

- Death of a beloved pet.

This isn't presented as a depressing message, it is presented as an inevitability. But this is also the first technique in dealing with it – an acceptance that it will happen. You can't change it, but you can find ways of dealing with it when it does.

The second way of dealing with it comes from this inevitability and affects our daily life. We have to love and treasure people and things whilst we have them. So whilst our loved ones are alive and our circumstances are good, we treasure them, knowing that they are temporary. If we knew we were going to lose them we would value them more. Well, we are going to lose them.

But this doesn't help us in the immediate

aftermath of the event. The trauma of the death notification or getting the news from the doctor isn't softened by the ultimate inevitability of the event. This leads to the next coping technique – how to deal with the initial shock.

First of all, don't deny how you feel. It is major, it is traumatic, and if you tell yourself anything different you are merely storing up problems for the future. This is when emotions go down into the basement and pump iron so they develop strength and come back later and take over. You have to deal with them and feel them when they arise.

Sometimes we will say things such as 'we have to be strong for the kids'. Why? What you're teaching them is that hiding emotions is a good thing, and then making them feel weak because they **do** have the emotions that you are hiding or denying. Would it not be better for their long-term development if they realized the inevitability of these events and also that it's okay to feel sad when someone dies?

Perhaps one of the reasons we struggle when these major life events happen is because we saw adults dealing with them by hiding their true feelings when we were young. We then acquired the 'knowledge' that this is the 'right' way and carried it into adulthood. Unfortunately though, it can lead to repressed feelings or unhelpful coping techniques. Well-meaning adults have, in effect, told us that feeling the way we do is somehow wrong or inappropriate.

Obviously you need to try and exercise some wisdom in these circumstances. You do need strength and resilience to cope with funeral arrangements and having an emotional child that you cannot help is not particularly helpful in this situation. When this happens you do sometimes have to send your feelings to the basement so that you can get on with other things. But don't beat yourself up when doing this, accept what you're having to do and acknowledge that you will need to find some personal emotional processing time when circumstances permit.

In the short-term, you need immediate coping techniques. Relaxation activities will be important, as will things that energise you, such as exercise or taking time in nature or to do a hobby. Psychological techniques can also help, such as hypnosis, which can give temporary relief for relaxation or 'mental protection' for dealing with a funeral or other key events. Know your own preferred techniques for relaxation and energising – you will need them at this time.

Another key technique to use both at this time and longer-term is to realize and think about what you still have, rather than what you've lost. Parents who lose a child will inevitably suffer great loss, but they may also neglect other children, family members or friends. These other parties then begin to feel unloved or live in the shadow of someone else or an event, which stunts their own development. Focusing on what we still have can also give us relief as we can take momentary pleasure in the things that are around us, rather than feeling depressed at what we've lost.

I'm always greatly troubled when I hear of people that want to end their lives due to physical illness. This is another example of focusing on what has been lost, rather than what we still have. Our bodies might not work as well as they used to, but our minds often still do, and we can use that for alternative activities instead. I'm not saying this is easy, but it is incredibly inspiring when we see someone else overcoming tremendous adversity. There are many stories of paraplegics who have written great literature or produced great art, or provided wisdom and hope for others. They are using what they have, rather than bemoaning what they've lost. The classic example is the cancer patient who cheers everyone up in the ward with their good humour and hopeful attitude.

As time goes on, you will need to process your emotions and accept them. Don't deny how you feel, go with it. Don't try to rush it though, otherwise you won't complete the task effectively, you need to take as long as it takes. What you're ultimately working towards is acceptance – both of the fact that it has happened and that life will be different from now on as a result. The old normal has gone, to make way for a new normal. But that's the key point – the old normal *won't* be coming back, no matter how much you want it. Accept that you have a new normal. You might not like the new normal, but it is what you have. The only way to ultimately deal with this is acceptance of it.

Seek out a support network to help you during this process. Speak to supportive friends and spend time with family members who can share how you feel. A good friend or compassionate family member will be glad to help you out. Remember though that you might have to actively seek them out as they won't necessarily know what's going on in your head. They might not realize that you need help – perhaps because you've been trying to appear strong.

You might also find that some people are afraid to come to you. Not because they don't care, but because they don't know what to do. They don't know what to say, or how to react. It might also bring up negative emotions for them that they aren't yet ready to address or that triggers painful memories. So tread carefully but let it be known that you need help and support, and the right people will find you. It might not be who you expect though, so be open to what presents itself. Your 'best friend' might not be of much help as they're caught up in their own trauma, but a neighbour or work colleague might be making themselves available, if you open to it.

Your resilience for coping with these events needs to be built up during the good times. Practising the techniques in this book or from other self-help techniques or religions will build up your strength, so that it is there when you need it. It can be hard to find the strength when trauma strikes, particularly if there are several in quick succession, so prepare in advance. This is also where an acceptance of the inevitability can help, because you know that these things will be presenting themselves at some point, so you're more ready when they do.

In time, you may find your strength building back up again. Having coped with the event, you will acquire greater understanding of how you responded, and greater wisdom of how to respond next time it happens to you or other people. It may even open up opportunities that would not have arisen otherwise, such as ways of helping people or types of voluntary work that you feel drawn towards. But take your time with this and don't bury yourself in distraction activities too often, you need to process it before you can move on.

I've found the book *The Mindful Path to Self-Compassion* by Dr Christopher Germer a great help in dealing with this process. The five stages in healing it presents were discussed in more depth in How Long Does it Take? in Chapter 7 – The Process Of Healing.

Areas for Contemplation

◆ Is there anyone or anything from your past for which you hold resentment? What feelings and sensations does thinking about it create for you?

◆ Could you forgive (release the anger or bitterness) the person(s) or event(s) that you perceive created the feeling? Is there anything holding you back from doing it? Could you do anything about it to move closer to the stage where you might be able to release some of the resentment?

◆ How easily could you submit to the power of the universe and release your need to control events and people?

◆ Do you live in the moment or are you always finding yourself ruminating on the past or planning the next event?

◆ Think of an act of kindness you have seen or received. How did you feel about it? Could you have done the same thing? What would stop you?

◆ The next time you feel the need or see the opportunity to do something for someone, do it without thinking. Afterwards, spend some time reflecting on your feelings around it by considering how you felt and what you were thinking before, during and after the event.

♦ Now think of a time when you could have acted but didn't. How does it make you feel to think back on it?

♦ Are there any groups for whom you would find it difficult to feel compassion? For example, murderers, rapists, junkies, paedophiles, terrorists? Spend some time trying to get into their head and thinking about why they might have done the actions they did. This isn't to try and justify their action, this is an exercise in learning more about yourself. Can you see any similarities between their actions and things you may have done? You might not have acted to the same degree, but is the *root* of the attitude similar, such as acting through anger, bitterness, jealousy or self-focus?

♦ How would you feel about volunteering to help out a group of strangers for no reward?

♦ Can you remember what your childhood passions were? Spend some time thinking about how you spent your time as a child and what you ***wanted*** to be doing. Were they different? Why? Was something stopping you that's no longer in place?

♦ If you could draw up the ideal but realistic life, what would it consist of? This isn't about fanciful hopes and dreams such as winning the lottery or suddenly having the health and energy to run a marathon, keep it realistic such as the job you would like or the hobbies you could take up. Identify the individual elements which constitute it, such as job or career, relationships, health improvements, type of activities, etc.

♦ What small actions could you take now or in the next few days to move slightly closer to achieving this 'ideal' picture? Will anything stop you? If so, how could you deal with it? Repeat this exercise and way of thinking for the next 2 months and then review how much closer you are to achieving the elements of this 'ideal' life. If you don't feel you've moved closer, reflect back over the previous two months and identify what stopped you doing the small actions. What could you have done differently? What could stop you doing it differently next month and how might you resolve it?

♦ Have you ever told someone that what they were planning to do was not a good idea? Were you stealing their dream? How did they react?

♦ Has anyone ever stolen your dream? Can you identify why they did it?

♦ Reflect back on some of the major life events you have experienced. How did you deal with them? Did you emotionally collapse under the strain or did you consider yourself to be strong? How could you have dealt with it differently?

Chapter 10

Therapy and Therapeutic Techniques

So far, we've looked at how we have become what we are and why the world is the way it is. Then we looked at how to change our view of the world so that it feels like a happier, more peaceful place - for us. We may or may not have changed anything in the outside world, but now we know that how we feel is dependent on what's going on inside us. Happiness is an internal thing so if we feel happy then we are, by definition, happy. We may have achieved this by changing how we view the world, or it may have involved making actual changes to our circumstances.

Real changes take place inside of us at the emotional and thinking level, but we can introduce helpers and enablers to facilitate the process along. Some of these are explored in this chapter and the next. They include areas such as therapy, complementary medicine, religion and rituals. A word of caution about them though; none of them provide 'cures'. The only 'cure' available to us is changing how we feel inside, although some techniques can help the process along a bit.

When we are ill, we take something to make ourselves feel better such as a pain killer. We can use therapeutic techniques in the same way. The secret to using them successfully lies in finding the right technique and the right therapist. They are sometimes referred to as 'alternative medicine' but the term 'complementary' is more accurate. Calling them 'alternative' implies an either/or approach, which isn't true. Western medicine is incredibly helpful and useful, and complementary techniques can greatly aid their effectiveness.

Although Western medicine has created some wonderful techniques such as painkillers, antibiotics and surgery, there are downsides to these advances. Western medicine tends to group together a set of symptoms into a disease or illness which can then be treated as if it were a 'thing'. This is a classic example of separation and discrimination dictating how we view the world.

But Western medical approaches generally treat the *symptoms* rather than the underlying cause. The net effect is that we are not cured, we merely feel better as a result of relief of the symptoms. Nothing wrong with that of course, but it can be superficial and emphasises the external nature of how we view the world, i.e. taking something from the outside – a drug – and applying it to an internal feeling such as pain and discomfort.

Ancient cultures and civilisations used plants and herbs to treat symptoms but it wasn't actually the plant as such that helped, it was some of the components of the plant, i.e. an active ingredient that created the effect. Modern medicine uses a similar approach in that it finds the active, effective ingredient but then manufactures it commercially together with a number of other ingredients into a delivery mechanism, such as a tablet or injection. These additional chemicals can have negative effects because we are introducing a foreign agent, i.e. a manufactured chemical, into our body and it might not like it – it creates an adverse reaction for which we might need to find additional symptomatic relief. Natural remedies have the active ingredient but not necessarily the extra chemicals and their side-effects.

But where the ancient cultures really had the edge was that they didn't just stop at the effective ingredient which treated the symptoms, they looked more holistically at the situation to find out what might have *caused* it, then also treated that. They looked for the cause of the disease, or perhaps more accurately the dis-ease - and treated that too, making the treatments more effective in the long run and aiding our general wellbeing. This is the origin of things such as shamanic practises that helped to ease a troubled soul or investigated the root of problems through dreams. By seeing what causes our dis-ease, we can make our lives more whole, complete and balanced, fueling more wellbeing in the future and aiding our happiness.

This is the principle behind many complementary therapies, in that they seek the cause of our dis-ease and help lead us to ways that make us more complete and generally happier. They may also be accompanied by natural remedies to provide symptomatic relief.

I have categorized complementary therapies into three broad groups; psychological, internal energy-based, and ancillary or sensory-based. These are not scientific or 'official' classifications, they are merely my shorthand way of presenting them.

Psychological

These are sometimes called 'talking therapies' but this is an incorrect label because most of the therapeutic aspects happen in our minds outside of the therapy session, with the talking aspect acting as a contributor. The therapist may actually do very little talking but instead might give us guidance on how our thinking patterns may be affecting us. The real work happens in our day-to-day lives outside the therapy room.

One of the most common forms of psychological therapy is cognitive-behavioural therapy, or CBT for short. CBT was discussed earlier in Thinking Patterns in Chapter 3 and can be incredibly valuable in helping us identify and address issues we may have. During a CBT session we will talk about our experiences, feelings and subsequent consequences, with the therapist probing for what might have caused it and suggesting alternative approaches. Outside of the therapy session we use mindfulness to identify what we are feeling and thinking, then try to use the alternative approaches discussed in the session. Over time we will start to experience improvements in how we feel and our reactions to the feelings. In the longer term, it is considered to be a more effective technique than drugs for conditions such as anxiety and depression but it can also be incredibly valuable for treating phobias, eating disorders and trauma effects.

A criticism of CBT is that it seeks coping mechanisms rather than addressing the causes, meaning that it provides a superficial approach to healing. This is probably true but is only an issue if the causes do actually need to be investigated. If I have a headache, I'll take a painkiller and it will go away. I don't need to investigate what caused the headache unless it becomes a recurring problem. Other psychological therapies may spend too long investigating deep-seated causes when all that's really needed is the equivalent of a painkiller to let the person get on with their life, or provide symptomatic relief whilst they investigate causes in more depth.

Another useful and valuable form of psychological therapy is hypnosis. Therapeutic hypnosis does not involve a hypnotist putting us into an unconscious trance and then planting suggestions in our mind. We are in full control with complete awareness during a hypnosis session. The hypnotist will not be using some magical, controlling powers to get us to do things against our will.

The principle behind therapeutic hypnosis is that many of our daily actions are actually guided by our subconscious mind. We are being provided with thoughts and emotions by our subconscious that make us act in certain ways, such as feeling fear, uncontrolled eating or smoking. By speaking directly to the subconscious mind we can break these automatic, uncontrolled reactions and 'cure' ourselves of the problem. We might have an emotional connection to food, for example, which means we eat for comfort but also when we feel good. So rather than viewing food as body-fuel, it provides an emotional crutch for us. Breaking the connection between food and emotion means we view food in a different way and naturally change our eating patterns as a result. With smoking we might train our subconscious that it wants to breathe in fresh, cool, calming air and that we are calm and strong, so we no longer feel the need for a cigarette.

Talking directly to the subconscious mind is done by going into a relaxed but fully aware state where we are amenable to alternative ways of doing things. We then use metaphor, imagery, language and visualization to encourage it to see the world in a different, more helpful way, meaning that it provides us with different messages. The subconscious mind is actually fairly dumb in the same way that a computer is, as it can only process and give back what is given to it. So if we give it good stuff, it will give us good things back. But if our upbringing means that it is full of harmful, unhelpful thinking, that's what we'll get.

Hypnosis can work very well alongside CBT. We can use CBT to identify the unhelpful thinking techniques we have, then use hypnosis to give us a 'booster' in changing these ways of thinking more quickly than if we only focus on our conscious thoughts and feelings.

It can also be very valuable in treating the effects of trauma. Trying to deal with a trauma and the subsequent effects by talking about it can be very counter-productive because we keep reliving the trauma and reinforcing the feeling. Hypnotic techniques mean that we can go directly to the subconscious mind and break the connection with the effects, meaning that we suffer less. It can't take the past events away, but it can help us to engage more effectively with our current life and get more out of it, rather than living with the effects and pain of the past.

Internal energy and sensory-based

This includes therapies such as acupuncture, Reiki, spiritual healing and shamanic practises but is an area that can get a bad reputation because of its lack of scientific proof. I believe this is as much due to misunderstanding as anything. There might not be any 'proof' as measured by Western scientific requirements, but there is actually some sound scientific logic behind it. The ultimate proof, though, is whether it helps us or not.

The effects of feelings such as stress, depression and anxiety on wellbeing and the body are well-known, but the mechanism of how the effects are created is not entirely understood by the Western scientific and medical communities. The concept of internal energy provides an explanation and therefore a solution to these conditions that we can use.

When we look at physical objects, or matter as it is called scientifically, we see it as solid. But any scientist will tell you that this is incorrect, it's just how we perceive it. Everything is made up of particles and atoms but within, and between them, lies empty space and energy. The atoms themselves are made up of sub-atomic particles and what lies between them is, guess what, empty space and energy. Sub-atomic particles are actually just massive bundles of energy flying around in patterns that we perceive as being 'solid.'

We can't see this energy but we can deduce that it's there from its effects. In the search for the Higgs Boson and other sub-atomic particles, for example, the scientists didn't actually see the particle, they saw the effects of its energy and drew conclusions accordingly. This is like seeing smoke coming from a chimney and deducing that there is a fire in the fireplace. We can't see the fire, but it must be there in some fashion otherwise there couldn't be smoke. This concept is actually at the root of many things we encounter in life, i.e. we can't see it directly, we have to deduce what's actually going on. You can't read someone's mind but you can deduce or guess what they might be thinking.

Because particles and atoms have their origins in energy, the entire universe must be made of energy, as are we. Energy-based healing methods tap into this energy and use it for positive effect within us. When we are stressed or anxious, our internal energy can be considered as not flowing as effectively as it could be and may even be blocked, as water might be blocked in a pipe. In the same way that energy is perceived as solid objects in our visible world, this internal energy manifests as feelings within ourselves and physical symptoms. We can't see the energy in either ourselves or atoms, but we can deduce that it must be there, like the smoke from a chimney indicating that there must be a fire in the hearth.

The concept of chakras can help us to understand how this internal energy works. Chakras are focal points within the body from which the energy can be considered as flowing from and between. If a chakra is blocked, i.e. energy isn't flowing smoothly through it, we will experience particular symptoms. For example, if we are feeling stressed or adrift or not feeling calm with our place in the world and perhaps holding ourselves very tight in an anxious manner as a result, we will feel back pain because the energy isn't flowing smoothly through our root chakra. In effect, we have a blocked energy pipe which we experience as physical pain and discomfort. Someone who has become attuned to internal energy can 'see' or feel how it flows within us and channel it in a more helpful way. So they may be able to help rebalance the chakra by unblocking the pipe and getting the energy flowing freely and smoothly again, meaning that we don't feel the back pain. But the treatment will not necessarily have been on any injury which might have led to the pain, it will have been on the sensation and feelings of pain and discomfort caused by it.

One point to bear in mind about chakras is that they are not physical objects within us like a liver or kidney, they are concepts used to demonstrate and illustrate where the main energy points lie. You can't have exploratory surgery and see a chakra, and you can't open up an atom and see its energy. But you can see the *effects* of the energy (like the Higgs Boson experiments or the smoke from the chimney) and deduce that it must be there as a result. Although you can't physically see a chakra, if you tune into your emotions and feelings you can sense the effects of it.

I can vouch for the efficacy of the internal-energy approach as I have used acupuncture and Reiki together for this very purpose, and no longer suffer so much from back pain – or anxiety. I also have an increased feeling of wellbeing and being at peace with the world. That's sufficient proof for me.

Looking deep within ourselves and finding the

root of our psychological issues and pain can have the same effect. Becoming more at peace with the world – getting in touch with our soul or true self – will in turn create more balanced energy flows and lead to physical improvements. A skilled therapist can help direct us to areas where we may be experiencing blockages in our life as well as giving a 'boost' to the healing process.

As you can imagine, this is an area that could lend itself well to lots of charlatans and conmen. Because we are unable to see and feel the energy and chakras ourselves, together with the lack of objective proof, it means that anyone can set themselves up as a 'healer', so vulnerable and desperate people may spend a lot of money and be conned. If you plan on using one of these techniques, be careful about which techniques and therapists you select. There needs to be a chemistry between you, otherwise the therapist or healer will not be able to tune into your energy and help you. Choose carefully.

It also helps to be in tune with your own emotions and feelings. The more aware you are of them, the greater the chance of the therapist picking up on it and being able to channel their activities more effectively. It also means that if you're not in tune, you may not feel immediate benefits. Unlike psychological therapy techniques, they don't work directly on how you think, they work on how you feel, so if you don't know how you feel, things might not seem much different from the way they were before. They will ultimately have an effect on how you think and view the world though, because feelings and emotions come first, before the conscious thoughts we are aware of.

Internal energy-based therapies are also like psychological therapies in that much of the healing actually takes place outside of the session afterwards. When you unblock your energy pipes and it starts flowing again, all sorts of emotionally painful memories, experiences and realizations can come up. Whilst a series of acupuncture sessions might do wonders for your sore back or other condition, unless you look at the cause of the condition – the source of the dis-ease – it will come back. So make sure you take time to think, contemplate and journal after sessions of energy-based healing, so you can make the fundamental changes in your life needed to prevent the condition coming back again. If you clear the water pipes in your house to remove blockages, you need to do something to prevent it happening again. Internal energy is the same. Not treating the cause of the blockage is only treating the symptoms, not the cause.

Some retreat centres, such as the Findhorn Foundation, have 'experience weeks' which bring lots of these psychological and energy-based techniques together in an intensive treatment, away from the distractions of day-to-day life. They can have dramatic effects in a short period, if we can give the time and money to doing it. But if we can't make that commitment, a regular programme such as a weekly or fortnightly acupuncture or Reiki session can also have rapid, dramatic effects on us at a lower cost.

Ancillary, sensory-based. There are a variety of other techniques that I call ancillary because they are unlikely to create dramatic changes within us but they can help the process along, or at least give some short-term relief such as relaxation or a pleasant experience. They include techniques such as Emotional Freedom Technique (EFT – sometimes called 'tapping' because it involves touch at specific points in the body), EMDR (eye movement desensitisation which is believed to work in a similar way to hypnosis), crystal therapy (which channels the energy of the earth via our chakras), aromatherapy and massage. I call them 'sensory-based' because they generally act on one or more of the senses, such as touch (massage) or scent (aromatherapy).

If you want to use any of these, the usual guidelines apply such as picking the right technique and therapist. The technique might depend on which sense you feel most strongly disposed towards. I'm more kinaesthetic (touch) and sound-based, so visually-oriented therapies don't really do a lot for me. Choosing the right therapist will also depend on the right surroundings, i.e. somewhere quiet and peaceful rather than a room in a house or beside a busy road, although some activities can be done at home such as burning candles or listening to a CD.

Journaling

As we start to investigate ourselves more deeply, we will need a way of recording what we come up with and may also feel the need to make changes to our life. If we are to stop acting in habitual, unhelpful ways, we need alternative approaches so it pays to have a method of recording these when they come up. Also, spending time dedicated to thinking about something and having to write down the conclusions creates a disciplined approach which can be helpful. Keeping a journal of your thoughts, feelings and actions can be done on a regular basis, such as daily, or alternatively it can be used when inspiration strikes.

When I was undergoing therapy I found it useful to write up a journal every day, and at times hourly, but now I tend to use it only when I have identified something significant. I may go two months or more without recording anything. I used journaling to help identify my hot thoughts and get a sense of what triggered them. It was also very useful for tracking progress towards a resolution.

A disconcerting experience I sometimes have is when I get a major flash of insight which I want to record but then see that the same thing happened 12 months ago. I'd forgotten it. So it helps to go back through your journal regularly and see what you have come up with. It may well be that you wrestled with the same issue six months ago but just didn't realize it as daily life took over. Another major advantage of revisiting what you've written in the journal is that it reminds you just how far you've come. Things which seemed like really big important issues several months ago may now have paled into insignificance. This is an important confidence booster on the journey.

One word of caution about using a journal: use it as a tool, not a stick with which to beat yourself. Whilst using a disciplined approach to journaling can be really useful, if you don't stick to the approach it can feel like a major chore when you return to it, but if you don't it might be another thing you add to your personal 'failure' list. When reading back over it you may also feel a sense of depression or frustration that you have been so silly in the past or are not making fast enough progress. So tread lightly, it needs to be a tool to help you, not another opportunity to condemn yourself. If it's not working for you, stop doing it.

Problem-solving and Decision-making

Journaling helps us to understand more about our feelings and record them, but problem-solving is needed to identify what's really going on and identify root causes. Decision-making is something we will have to do as a result but it needs wisdom and understanding to be done effectively.

The key to solving any problem is investigation. Too often we will jump to conclusions on something without having fully investigated all the facts related to it. In our action-focused, achievement-oriented modern society, quick decision-making and the ability to think on our feet are often praised as 'good things'. When we are being chased by a sabre-toothed tiger or in a combat situation this skill is indeed helpful, but for most decisions and situations it's actually very dangerous. Sensible decision-making and problem-solving needs a measured, calculated response using a combination of investigation, logical conclusions, intuitive reasoning and emotional feelings.

When faced with a situation that does not need an immediate response, i.e. you're not about to be eaten by a tiger or crash the car, then start with the principles of PRADA and RAIN. Stop, slow down and investigate. Use the full range of investigative techniques, including logical conclusions and past experiences, to try and understand what has caused it, your role in it and what the consequences of different solutions might be. Take as long as needed for this, there are very few things that you can't sleep on first.

As part of the investigation, ask the specific question of how long the issue is likely to be a problem for. Ask specifically; 'will this still be a problem in 1 hour, 1 day, 1 week, 1 month or 6 months?'. The answer will give a sense of perspective on the scale of the problem. For example, if it is unlikely to be a problem tomorrow then it is only a problem for today so all you need is some patience and it will go away naturally by itself shortly. On the other hand, if not acting on it today means that it will still be a problem next week or next month whereas it can be resolved today and remove the issue for the future, then you have a solution. What a wonderful approach to procrastination.

When you have analysed the situation and know the reasons for it and have an idea of some potential consequences, assessed logically and calmly, you can move into the decision-making phase. As mentioned when discussing PRADA, there are actually likely to be very few potential solutions available to you. Generally you can either change the situation or accept it. Decision-making usually means deciding first of all whether a change should be made or if it actually needs acceptance instead, and then which particular change option to take, if applicable.

Start off the process by working through as many consequences as you can for each change option. It can help to state the options on a sheet of paper and then write down the consequences of each option. This in itself will often be enough to illustrate which option is the best choice but there is something very important that needs to be introduced at this stage. When you look at this logical conclusion, does it *feel* right? Can you feel in your bones, heart and skin that it is the right thing to do? Are you sure? If it is, then the decision has been made. You will feel a 'resonance', it will naturally feel like the right thing to do. If there is something that doesn't *feel* quite right, regardless of the logical conclusion, you need to look further.

This is where the emotional aspect of decision-making comes into it. This 'feeling' is really important. If the decision resonates, your heart and mind will be in it. If it doesn't, then you need to investigate what it is about the decision that doesn't feel right. You could go back to your journal and see if there is anything in there that indicates why it might not feel right, or you might want to think about it for a bit longer. It might be a past memory of things going a certain way and deep down you feel that an option might take you down the same path again, or it could be a habitual fear that's holding you back. If you have attuned yourself to your emotions you may also begin to feel the areas of your body which are expressing the discomfort, thus highlighting the emotional aspect you are unsure of.

Sometimes the options will feel the same and you have nothing to differentiate between them, neither logical conclusions nor emotional feelings. In this case the solution is not very scientific but it is highly effective; toss a coin. This isn't so that you make decisions based on chance. Decision-making on this basis might be a fun exercise for developing spontaneity and reducing control needs, but it's very dangerous for anything significant. The importance of the result of the toss is that it forces out a decision which you can then assess to see whether it feels right or not. If it feels right, if it has resonance, then emotionally it is the right thing to do. If it doesn't feel right, pick the other alternative and see if that has resonance instead.

Either way, forcing a decision makes you identify which has resonance and thus brings out the more emotional, intuitive aspects of the decision, meaning you choose actions which have both a sensible logical component and that are closer to your emotional values. In time, you will learn to identify these aspects of decisions more readily, leading to more rounded, balanced choices without the need for an external stimulus to force it out. But you shouldn't blindly follow the decision because the coin said so. It's not about following a rule, it's helping you get more in touch with emotional feelings so that they can help inform decision-making.

Areas for Contemplation

- ♦ What's your reaction to the thought of therapy or 'healing' of any kind? Do you feel you should be able to handle things and events yourself or are you open to assistance?

- ♦ What forms of therapy do you feel most drawn towards? Why?

- ♦ Are there any current issues that you feel a form of therapy could help with? Which type?

- ♦ Find a notepad that appeals to you and start

keeping a journal. Write anything in it that you wish and then make a point of writing something every day. Anything will do, even if it's random doodles.

♦ After a month, look through your journal and review what you've written. Has it reminded you of anything you'd forgotten about? Think about how a journal would help you and adopt that practise as a habit from now on.

♦ How do you normally make decisions? Are they quick and hasty, or long thought-out processes with the application of logic, or do you use intuition and gut-feel?

♦ The next time you are faced with a decision, use additional techniques to aid the process. So if you are logical, try scanning your body to identify if there are any physical sensations that arise when you think about the elements of the decision. If you use gut-feel or emotions, take some time to write down the consequences of each option available to you.

Chapter 11

Regular Practises and Activities

Meditation is an incredibly useful practise that essentially involves being sat on your backside thinking about things. It can be focused, i.e. thinking about something specific to deepen your understanding of it or discover where it came from, or unfocused, so that you observe what you're thinking about it. Both approaches help you to know yourself better and identify what your delusions and virtuous thoughts are. Then you can do something about them.

Another major benefit of meditation is the peace and quiet it brings, which in itself is hugely appealing and beneficial. A short period of peace and silence helps us recharge and reflect in our hectic lives. It is also a fundamental component of the stopping-calming-resting-healing sequence. Calming and resting come from meditation and can only happen when we stop what we're doing, which then leads to healing.

So how do you do it? Basically, just sit down and shut up, perhaps with your eyes closed to reduce the potential for distractions. It needn't be anything more complex than that. One thing you'll notice when you start doing it is how active your mind seems to be. It will flit from thought to thought, possibly with no apparent connection between them. Many people think this means they can't meditate or that it makes their mind even busier than usual. Neither is true.

First of all, this is how busy your mind always is, it's just that you've never noticed before. It's the act of stopping for meditation that gives you the opportunity to finally see what's always been happening but that you've never really been aware of – that your mind is full of stuff and continually sending you messages and talking to you. The awareness of our busy mind is the starting point of mindfulness, or being aware of what's in our mind at any one moment. Is it full of anger and jealousy, or is it calm and peaceful?

Secondly, it's not possible to not be 'good' at meditating. There's no achievement involved and it's not a skill to learn. It's something private to yourself, all yours, that no-one can ever take away and that you can do anything you want with. It is beneficial to learn how to still the mind and increase concentration, but take it slowly and gently – it's not supposed to be a challenge.

Start with just a couple of minutes at first and concentrate on your breathing. Feel your breath coming into your body and then back out again. Keep doing this until you notice that your mind has drifted off (you'll notice after about 20 seconds that it drifted off 18 seconds ago), then start becoming aware of your breath again. Repeat as often as you like. When you feel ready and willing, you can start thinking about specific things, either a problem you currently face, or some of the points from this book, or anything else. Or you can just sit and relax, enjoying the peace and quiet for a moment.

We make better decisions when we are mindful. If we can see that our mind is angry, it might not be the best time to confront the person who 'made' us angry. So we stop and reflect on the situation before deciding on the wisest course of action. Perhaps we might start to see the situation from their side and realize that they are actually lashing out because of frustration at something **we** have done or that has happened to them. Rather than perpetuating the conflict, we might then have compassion for **their** suffering, so we apologise and help them instead.

Or we might take the time to see what is really causing our discomfort. We might think that our boss is a horrible bully but using mindfulness we notice the real problem is that we don't actually like our job and this causes our performance to deteriorate. The bullying is then the manager's way of dealing with the situation we have caused. Granted, it's not a particularly clever way of dealing with it, but the real problem – for us - is that we don't like the job, rather than the manager's personality. We might then decide to train for another career better suited to our personality and interests, or find a new job.

Mindfulness is a moment-by-moment practise

and meditation is something that we make time for, but both require us to stop what we're doing and do something else instead, which is not particularly helpful if we're walking, driving, shopping or working. Awareness allows us to bring the principles of mindfulness more into our daily lives.

The opposite of awareness is self-focus. When we're caught up in ourselves or what we're doing it's very difficult to hear the birds singing, or smell the flowers, or see the person around us that needs help. We are closed to what is happening around us or to anything outside of our selves. Then something might intrude into our consciousness and we get a fright, which might lead to anger and blaming someone else for disturbing or scaring us. Awareness means using a little bit of our consciousness to see and feel what's happening around us, leaving our senses free to see, smell, hear and realize what's going on. It might be external sounds or smells, or internal feelings and sensations that alert us to something happening. It might be seeing people around us and observing them, so that we see what they are doing and can, in effect, anticipate what might happen next.

Walking along the street we might see someone in front of us texting on their phone and not looking where they are going. If we are doing the same we might bump into them, but observing and being aware means we see the danger in advance and steer clear. By being more aware we also see what we might be doing that is affecting other people. Perhaps we might see that our lack of attention is actually starting to create a little bit of frustration in someone else. Then we can alter what we're doing to ease the situation before it becomes an issue.

This type of awareness can also give us great joy because we see so much more of life going on around us. We can take pleasure in so many other things that we might never have noticed and we may have the opportunity to avoid some problems before they even arise. It can be built up on an ongoing basis just by noticing how aware we are of what's going on around us and trying to do more of it. Developing greater ongoing awareness will also help us with meditation and mindfulness as they become easier – both things benefit enormously from it.

You can start increasing your awareness right now by listening to what you can hear and what you can smell. Is there a bird singing in the background or is it the sound of keyboards clicking, phones ringing or traffic? Can you smell freshly cut grass or the cup of coffee or glass of wine in front of you? Are you warm or cold? Comfortable or uncomfortable? Who is around you right now and how do they appear to you? Do they seem stressed and agitated or calm and peaceful? Can you have this awareness whilst you're doing something else, such as reading or watching the television? Whenever you remember, try to be more aware and over time the skill will increase so that you get more out of every single moment you are alive, rather than being pre-occupied with your troubles and not noticing anything else.

Someone with highly-developed, moment-by-moment general awareness skills can appear to be psychic, because of their uncanny ability to know what's going on and what might happen next.

Rituals

Rituals can take a variety of forms and be for a number of purposes. They are particularly useful for symbolising a change, such as forgiveness, or the closing of a chapter in our lives. When we do a ritual for these things, it's as if it emphasises in our mind the change we are making and gives it greater strength.

A ritual for forgiveness, for example, could involve writing down the things for which we hold anger or bitterness and then burning the paper. The fire symbolises the end of an attitude by transforming it into something else – the flames and smoke, leaving only ashes behind which we might then put on the garden to provide extra nutrients for it. We have recycled the feelings into something else. We might also read out the thing that we are burning, so that it becomes more real for us, and then the old feeling dissipates into the air.

Another useful area for rituals is disposing of unhelpful ways of thinking. I once put soil, dirt and stones into a bag, took it to the seaside and poured it into the sea. The meaning behind this was disposing of the old rubbish – the unhelpful ways of thinking about things and putting them into something else. After carrying the excess baggage around for a while, I got rid of it - literally. I obviously had to do a lot of work on my own feelings afterwards to reinforce it, but the ritual helped to cement the action by allowing me to visualize and feel what I was doing.

As well as symbolising a point of change, rituals can also be used as a way to reinforce thinking patterns that we want to develop more of. Many religious-based rituals are of this form. The Christian Eucharist, for example, doesn't mean that the bread and wine are physically transformed into Jesus' body and blood. Instead it reminds worshippers by means of a ceremonial ritual that Jesus died for their sins. Worshippers can then carry this reinforcement and reminder into their daily lives by trying to embody and internalize the feelings and attitudes it created within themselves.

Attending a regular religious service can also have a similar effect. It isn't really that there is a set of rules we have to follow and if we don't we will be struck down or doomed to eternal damnation. It's also not the case that some external deity – a God – will look kindly on us for going and give us a little pat on the head for doing so. It's more about providing a regular reminder of a way of living that is more helpful than our usual worldly, self-focused basis.

Before condemning rituals as superstitious nonsense, look at what they are really trying to teach. People who have an altar at home, for example, may make prayers or prostrations to a statue and then make the area beautiful with fresh flowers and offerings on a daily basis. This doesn't necessarily mean that they're looking for the metaphorical pat on the head from an external source. The act of praying or prostrating may instead be a reminder that there is something bigger than us, an ideal to strive for. It teaches humility, rather than self-focus. The offerings teach us to think of others rather than ourselves all the time, by spending a little bit of time doing something that's not purely for us. We can then carry these reminders into our daily lives, reinforcing them over time and moving us forward.

We can use established psychological rituals (such as the example of emptying a bag of stones into the sea, or writing down our grievances and then burning them), or those of a religious practise, or we can create our own. Creating our own ritual makes it personal and gives us a stronger, ongoing reminder than simply following what someone else says. I created symbolic rituals for myself that involved doing childhood activities (such as making chocolate crispy-cakes or colouring-in) to symbolise things that I wasn't able to do in childhood. This reminds me that many of my delusions and hang-ups came from childhood but as an adult I don't have to follow them. I can if I want, but I don't have to – I can take personal responsibility for my own feelings and actions. So if I want to do 'childish' activities, I can.

A regular ritual I have which comes from Buddhism but has similarities with Christian traditions is saying a little prayer before I eat. Christianity would call this 'saying grace', but in Buddhism it's an offering. I mentally offer what I'm eating to the hungry spirits, that they find food, water, peace of mind and shelter as a result of my good fortune. I don't really expect any 'hungry spirits' to eat as a result of what I say, but it does remind me that I am fortunate to live in a country where we have enough to eat, clean water, decent housing and wealth beyond the wildest imaginings of the majority of people on the planet. We don't live under a brutal dictatorship, our children aren't taken away as child soldiers and our female family members aren't subject to rape as a weapon of war. Saying an offering reminds me of my relative good fortune and teaches me gratitude for it, rather than enhancing my self-focus.

The ritual of 'namaste' is another which can be done on an ongoing, frequent basis. The word itself is from Sanskrit and is a greeting used between two people on the Indian subcontinent and generally throughout Asia. The full ritual involves putting our hands together at our chest as if praying whilst giving a little bow, but as with all rituals the actions themselves are much less important than the meaning behind it.

An extended meaning of namaste is 'the god in me greets the god in you'. This actually has incredible power behind it. First of all, it creates a feeling of equality between us; as two gods meeting each other, neither of is more important than the other but neither are we any *less* important than the person we are greeting. If we suffer from low self-esteem then we elevate ourselves to god-like status. But if we are arrogant and proud then we are reminded that we are talking to a god, which is very humbling. If we are judgmental then we will have hard time judging the person we are talking to – they are a god, after all.

A simple word with great meaning. Imagine saying "namaste" silently but mentally and without the physical gesture to every single person we came across. How much more harmonious our work meetings could be if we greeted all participants individually, giving them due credit for the god they are or could become. Think of the positive energy and compassion as a person with the power and status of a god we could bring to a group or an individual. We might not actually have that kind of power, but as with all rituals it's about what it's teaching us. Over time it will teach us equality, respect for others and not to be so judgmental.

Another phrase with great power is "Inshallah". Again, we can do it silently so that no-one ever knows we say it. Although descended from Arabic and traditionally used as an Islamic saying, variations of it are used throughout Spain, Portugal and the Balkans. The literal meaning is; "If god wills it" and it is used in situations where we are making plans for the future. So we could say "I'll see you tomorrow, inshallah", meaning "I hope to see you tomorrow, but it's not actually under my control whether I will or not, but it is my plan". What a fantastic way to reduce our control needs and increase acceptance that life will not always go the way we want. I heard a phrase once that had a similar meaning but doesn't quite trip off the tongue quite so easily; "if you want to give God a laugh, tell him your plans".

A Buddhist ritual that helps to reduce our discrimination is called Touching the Earth and was the final action the Buddha took before he achieved enlightenment. There are three stages involved in the ritual.

The first stage – the first touching of the earth – is to remind ourselves that we are part of a continuous chain. We were born to our parents and picked up many of their views and ways of living from them, as they in turn got theirs from our grandparents. We will continue this process by what we give to our younger people and the role models we are for them.

The second touching of the earth is to symbolise everyone around us now. In our daily lives we interact and affect people in the same way that they affect us. We are all interlinked and interdependent and this reminds us of the fact. It helps us to reduce our discrimination and judging, and instead aim for understanding and acceptance. Our thoughts lead to our actions which creates a ripple effect stretching out to everyone who encounters the result of that action. We also experience the results of other's actions which arises from their thoughts, which in turn comes from their experiences. This second touching reminds us of these interactions and connections, which we both give and receive.

The third touching of the earth represents a spiritual dimension so will not necessarily always be practised, if we don't feel that way inclined. We are part of a world of energy and spirit, sometimes manifesting in visible or physical form, sometimes not. These spirits and energy are there for us when we need them, to call upon for help and guidance. By getting more in tune with them and opening to what they have to say, we become more peaceful, centred and grounded within ourselves. We can take comfort in the fact that there is something bigger and more powerful than us, looking out for us.

Practising the three touchings of the earth (or just the first two if we're not spiritually inclined) reminds us of our place in the world together with the historical, present and (possibly) spiritual dimensions. By touching something solid as we do it, the earth, it helps to ground the feeling. We might visualize our parents and ancestors, our current world and our spiritual guides as we do each touching, so that the feeling becomes more powerful and stronger in our minds.

Religion and Spirituality

Many people find that having a religious faith gives them strength and meaning in life. It's also the case that it doesn't really matter which religion, it's the faith in a bigger picture that helps. For others, a belief in something that can't be proven is madness and has no place in the logical modern world.

I have both positive and negative views of religion. My main concern is about organised religions. At the core of most major religious beliefs is love and compassion for our fellow human beings. They express a hopeful message, one that gives us a way to relate to the world. The original masters or prophets of most religions, such as Jesus or Buddha, emphasise this message by providing teachings that help us live our lives.

The problems start when people get involved and bring human delusions into it. Jesus, for example, taught us to love our neighbour through parables such as The Good Samaritan, which helps us to frame how we deal with others. He taught us to look within ourselves and find our true selves – God or the Holy Spirit - and connect with it. But when humans misinterpret the messages and start to externalize them, they judge, control and try to convert others and force an approach on them, thinking that it is the 'one truth'. Nations will even go to war and kill or enslave others to bring 'the truth' to them.

A classic example of this is the Islamic concept of Jihad, which can be translated as 'holy war', but could equally well be translated as 'internal struggle'. It is a holy war, but *internal to ourselves*. It is about finding our *own* delusions, the things that take us further from love and then working with them so that we find more peace. This is the conflict it refers to, the one we have inside ourselves like the two wolves discussed earlier, or good versus evil. But apply external thinking to it and we will see *others* as good or evil, so that we then judge and try to control them. The teaching is actually encouraging us to look *inside ourselves* to root out the *internal* 'evil', not outside in the world.

As humans we could externalize the tale of the two wolves and see the world as literally a battle between two wolves, which would require a belief in something that can't be proven or seen. Or we could internalize it and use it to help us see how we *relate* to the world instead. Take the teachings of the ancient masters such as Jesus and apply this way of thinking to it. Remove the concept of an external God and instead relate it to our life and see how the message changes for you. The phrase 'forgive them, for they know not what they do' takes on a whole new context if Jesus isn't talking to an external entity but is instead removing bitterness from his own heart, so that he can die in peace and leave a powerful, lasting legacy with his last breath. Accept that the story of Adam and Eve isn't history but is a parable to demonstrate the cause and effect nature of the world we live in. Perhaps it is a story about the dangers of following a course of action without thinking through the potential consequences of it, rather than a history lesson.

Another example is how we relate to god and the devil. These can be seen as internal concepts – our loving god-like nature, versus the anger, bitterness and jealousy that arises from self-focus. Or we could externalize it and see both god and the devil as external entities – people, in effect. As humans, we tend to externalize things, rather than looking inside ourselves.

Remember that the original religious stories were verbal ways of demonstrating to people what was helpful and what wasn't, in a time when verbal storytelling was the predominant means of communication. Take it as literal history and you'll struggle. Take it as a teaching method, which is what they were originally designed as, and they can be incredibly helpful.

If we take religious teachings as something related to our inner soul, our heart, we can get immense comfort and knowledge from them. Not necessarily from the organized religion itself, but from the core teaching message. If we try to apply the teaching and messages to an external entity we will get caught up in concepts of proof, faith and trying to control the external world. But from the perspective of internal meaning, it doesn't really matter which religion we follow. If we look for the core teachings and put them in context, then apply them to *us* and how *we* feel rather than externalizing it, many of them have very similar messages. Then, if we like having a framework for the world and a support community, our religion can provide it but without getting caught up in problematic areas such as faith in something which cannot be proven to modern scientific standards.

Areas for Contemplation

♦ Take some time now to be aware of what's going on in your surroundings. Stop what you're doing and listen, look, feel. What are you aware of? Is there anything you notice now that you didn't before? Whenever you remember, take a moment to listen, look, feel and see what comes up.

♦ When you next can, stop and concentrate on your breathing for a few moments. Could you do it for long? What was going through your mind before you realized that you were no longer concentrating on your breath? Whenever you remember or get the opportunity, repeat the exercise.

♦ Could you build in a regular time to meditate every day, even if only for a couple of minutes? When would suit you best? Would it be the morning when you get up, or at lunchtime so that you get a break, or in the evening, perhaps immediately before bedtime? Try alternative times of the day or in different circumstances so that you build up a picture of when suits you best.

♦ Are you superstitious? Why?

♦ Are you facing any current issues where a ritual may help? Is there anything from your past that you are holding on to which could be released or eased by a personal ritual?

♦ Did any of the rituals discussed in this chapter touch you? Why?

♦ What was your childhood experience of religion? Did it put you off for life or was there anything about it that felt worthwhile?

♦ Could an organised religion play a part in your life?

♦ Have you seen or heard anything about any religions that appealed to you? Which aspects and why?

The 4 Noble Truths

How to Solve all our Problems !!

The 'Four Noble Truths' was the first teaching given by the Buddha after he achieved enlightenment. It is an incredibly powerful but simple concept that can change our whole life and how we feel about it. It doesn't need faith in anything or a belief in Buddhism, it is straightforward, ancient advice that we have forgotten in our busy, hectic, achievement-oriented modern lives.

The first truth is that to be alive is to encounter suffering. We think that if only we do the right things and follow the rules of life, everything will be okay. We are brought up to expect certain things – job, career, happy relationships, supportive family, etc. and if we work hard we can have it all. Unfortunately this just isn't true. We will have to put up with things and people we neither want nor like, we won't always get we want or expect, we'll get sick and die. And so will our loved ones. Get used to this; it's not going to change.

This in itself is incredibly powerful because it teaches us acceptance, rather than developing anger and bitterness at all the hardships and apparent unfairness we encounter.

The second truth is that our suffering has a

cause – us. It's our own actions and reactions that cause us to suffer. We can't stop the unpleasant things happening, but we can change our reactions to them so that we don't suffer so much as a result. You will find contented, optimistic disabled people, and miserable but wealthy able-bodied individuals surrounded by loving families with everything that others can only dream of. So it's not really our circumstances that cause the problems, it's how we deal with them.

The third truth is that because our suffering has causes, it also has solutions. We're not fixed, unchanging people, we are continually evolving and adapting. So our changes need to be to ways that bring us happiness and contentment, rather than anger, bitterness and depression. We can feed the internal happy wolf, making it stronger.

The fourth truth explains the path to changing how we feel, thereby bringing us peace, happiness and contentment. It won't necessarily bring us wealth and good health for us and all our loved ones, but it will reduce the suffering we experience from the inevitable difficulties that life brings us. Buddha called this path the 'Noble Eightfold Path' and the wisdom contained within it is the ancient teachings that show us a better way to live our lives. This is also what psychology, therapy and the core of many religions are also showing us.

We might read the first truth and think of it as

a depressing message, but it isn't, the four taken together are actually very hopeful and optimistic, when you truly understand them. They don't promise to take away the things that cause us problems, we will still have to cope with sickness, death, the actions of others and the consequences of our own actions. But they will reduce the suffering we *feel* as a result of them.

They tell us that we have a way out, a way to bring happiness and peace to our lives that is completely within our control.

What could be more powerful, optimistic, and full of hope than that?

Acknowledgements and References

A recurring theme throughout this book is that our life is created from the consequences of our actions and those of others, plus our reactions to the events and people that come into our life. Growth and development does not happen when things are going well for us, it happens when we perceive things have gone wrong and then have to do something about it. This is when we learn about our true selves and what motivates us or pushes our buttons.

So I firstly acknowledge the role of the bullies and the apparently heartless or self-focused individuals and groups I have encountered in my life. Without you and the lessons learned in response, this book would not have been possible, or indeed required. But as I have progressed through life I realize that these actions were not deliberately selfish or heartless, they were merely a response to the events and consequences of their own life.

We receive what we give, so I also acknowledge and apologise for the times when I too have been controlling and self-focused and made life difficult for others. Sorry.

My wife Mandy has been my soulmate, mentor and savior, plus she has typed and prepared this manuscript. I shall be forever grateful for all you have done for me, and continue to provide me with. Thank you.

Many teachers and guides have provided me with inspiration and some of them are listed in this section. Each of you has altered my life in fundamental ways with your writing and messages and for that I am truly grateful. Special mention goes to Geshe Kelsang Gyatso who has created a wonderful network of Buddhist retreat centres and teachings which has shown me a different, more peaceful and calm way of living.

I also want to mention my CBT therapist Val for the invaluable guidance she gave me at the start of my journey when I was struggling with anxiety. You really have changed my life.

I am especially grateful to some of the other therapists I have worked with who have helped me in so many ways, including Simon Bailey of the Navitas Reiki Centre, Julie Qin's Chinese Acupuncture and Roo Reygan who provides shamanic teaching and guidance.

And to my dear friend Ray Murphy who has now sadly passed away. Thank you for the chats and time, you will be forever in my heart.

Grateful acknowledgement is given for the titles below which have been drawn on for the production of this text. A full list of other helpful and contributing resources can be found on the accompanying website www.finding-peace.co.uk.

Canfield, J., Hansen, M. V. (1993) *Chicken Soup for the Soul*. London: Vermilion.

Chodron, P. (2010). *Taking the Leap: Freeing ourselves from old habits and fears*. Boston: Shambhala.

Foundation for Inner Peace (2007) *A Course In Miracles*. Mill Valley, CA: Foundation for Inner Peace.

Foster, J. (2012). *The Deepest Acceptance: Radical Awakening in Ordinary Life*. Boulder: Sounds True.

Germer, C. (2009). *The mindful path to self-compassion: Freeing yourself from destructive thoughts and emotions*. New York: The Guilford Press.

Gibran, K. (1991). *The Prophet*. London: Pan Macmillan.

Hough, M. (2010). *Counselling Skills and Theory*. Abingdon: Hodder Education.

Kornfield, J. (2008). *The Wise Heart: Buddhist psychology for the West*. London: Rider.

Kornfield, J. (2000). *After the Ecstacy, the Laundry; How*

the Heart Grows Wise on the Spiritual Path. London: Rider.

Miguel Ruiz, Jr. (2013). *The Five Levels of Attachment: Toltec wisdom for the modern world*. London: Hay House.

Nhat Hanh, T. (2010). *Reconciliation: Healing the Inner Child*. Berkeley: Parallax Press.

Nhat Hanh, T. (1991). *Peace is Every Step: The Path of Mindfulness in Everyday Life*. London: Rider.

Peck, M. S. (2006). *The Road Less Travelled*. London: Arrow Books.

Printed in Great Britain
by Amazon

61702642R00142